LOGO

R · I · P

The Stone Twins

CONTENTS

PREFACE

Welcome to the fully updated and revised second edition of *Logo R.I.P.* Readers of the original book, will notice that several things have changed in this new version. All articles were substantially rewritten, and, in some cases, were replaced by more compelling or current examples. But what has not changed is the core thesis of this book: that defunct logos – that were once an integral part of the landscape, our visual culture and our lives – are worthy of commemoration, or even preservation.

We wish to thank all the people who took the time to share their ideas on the website *logorip.com*, since its launch in 2003. This online 'Book of Condolences', or digital repository, provided a wealth of new material. It's a platform where fellow designers advocate for the preservation of iconic logos and critically discuss the merits of our funerary homage.

Just as importantly, the forum also attracted input that reveals the human cost of discarded logos: those individuals who lost their jobs, and are the fallout of corporate euphemisms, such as downsizing, restructuring, consolidation, repositioning or merger (the very terms that accompany the launch of shiny new trademarks). In addition, the website reveals the strong emotional bonds that ordinary people have with logos, and how they can trigger heated discussions on a variety of topics: from the environment (BP) to racism (Robertson's) or corporate loyalty (Wellcome), amongst others. The overall quality and scope of the comments on *logorip.com* enriched our understanding of the subject and provided a fresh impulse to refine, sharpen and update many of the 'obituaries'.

We take advantage of this opportunity to include several logos that have suffered an ignominious death, since the first edition in 2003. The ubiquitous and historic corporate symbols of Abbey National, AT&T, DSM, Hoechst, Kodak, Lucent, Rover, Unilever and Xerox have all been consigned to the logo graveyard. No revision of *Logo R.I.P.* could ignore the significance of these trademarks and the calls for their inclusion.

This fully revised version of *Logo R.I.P.* is also an acknowledgment of the growing movement to document the cultural and design history of trademarks; particularly icons from the golden era of corporate identity design (1950s to the 1970s). The preservation of our visual culture is central to our hypothesis; and echoes the goals of the architectural conservation movement. Some will argue that logos are just marks on paper and, inherently, ephemeral – but that's beside the point. As stated in our original introduction, great logos are much more than graphic marks that symbolise ideas or represent organisations. Logos hoard our memories, passions and reputations.

Besides, the great work of great designers is worthy of preservation. The graphic marks included in this book have significance every bit as important as landmark architecture. In recent years, this idea has been embraced by the writings of Michael Bierut[1] and Scott Stowell.[2] *Logo R.I.P.* has also inspired several exhibitions, most notably *L.I.P. (Logo in Peace)* at the Chaumont Poster Festival in 2010, and the series of *Dead Brands* events hosted by AIGA since 2009.

Furthermore, no update of this book could disregard the Global Financial Crisis of the late-2000s, which is considered by many economists to be the worst financial downturn since the Great Depression. A period that has seen the collapse of financial behemoths, such as Lehman Brothers and Washington Mutual – and contributed to the demise of household brands such as Kodak and Woolworths. The failure of these businesses, and the subsequent retirement of their visual signifiers, is one of the recurring themes in this book. With the pace of corporate funerals set to pick up further, many more titans of logo design look set to take their final bow. So, don't put away the black garb yet.

In short, *Logo R.I.P.* is as relevant as ever. Acknowledged as both a critique of corporate culture and a celebration of some of the most potent logos ever created – we invite you once again to take a moment to pause and reflect on our selection of lost logos that are, quite simply, well-conceived, well-crafted and well-known. Gone but not forgotten.

'Logo R.I.P.'

Declan and Garech Stone, The Stone Twins
Amsterdam, May 2012

FOREWORD

By keeping memories alive of things that happened in the past, one defines some sort of civilisation. In most cases, this is done in the form of a memorial such as a statue, an arch or a column. Graveyards too are places of reflection and act as a beacon of the collective memory.

This book is a commemoration of historical logos that have passed away. No one likes funerals, but in *Logo R.I.P.* there are many valuable trademarks that should be remembered, not just for today's generation of designers but also for the next.

The selection contained in *Logo R.I.P.* reveals the optimism, skill and craftsmanship of some great classic trademarks and logos. Apart from the functionality of these marks, which represent services and trades, these logos conjure up emotional responses – which range from the depraved (the Swastika) to the ingenuous (Spratt's).

This book is an important alternative to the new trend in logo design that is marketing-orientated nonsense. Many of today's solutions are produced by agencies that consist of a ratio of ten pin-stripes to every one creative. They are strategy-driven and lack stylistic durability, are missing concept, magic, wit, emotion or narrative – some of the major ingredients of a good logo. This marketing-driven fever of clients ultimately leads to nothing, producing bland future brands. Metaphorically speaking, these agencies are the 'gravediggers' for many design classics.

I hope, and sincerely wish, that this book becomes a valuable design resource in the future. Let's not make this a coffee-table book!

Gert Dumbar, Studio Dumbar
Rotterdam

INTRODUCTION

GONE BUT NOT FORGOTTEN: THE THANKLESS LIFE OF A REJECTED LOGO
Like it or not, logos are everywhere. In addition to the spine of this book, there's probably one emblazoned on your watch, sleeve, spectacles, shoes and coffee cup. Logos adorn almost every item in our vicinity, screaming their message, clamouring for attention.

Logos are signs, small graphic identifiers; things that help differentiate a product or service from its competitors. Yet over time, their meaning has transcended mere differentiation. Like personal signatures, logos are unique statements of their origins. They give away our background, our interests, our vanity and vulnerabilities. They mock our lifestyles, tell our income, betray our sociopolitical point of view.

And still they're so much more. Logos hoard our memories, passions and reputations. Made familiar with time, we come to trust and befriend them. Then, like mates, we give them nicknames (the 'Swoosh', 'Worm' or 'Piper'). In naming a logo, we infuse it with meaning, it helps classify and define who we are. In short, it helps us be.

Then one day, they desert us. They rust, fade from billboards, are replaced by new italicised upgrades.

BACKGROUND

Two years ago, when we began this book, our hypothesis was based on first-hand experience. We were submerged in a project based on the logo of pharmaceutical giant SmithKlineBeecham. Though we hadn't created this trademark, our task was to devise a corporate identity program for its application. Then just as we reached the implementation stage, it was announced that the entire project was to be dropped. The reason was simple: SmithKlineBeecham had agreed to a merger with arch rival GlaxoWellcome. The new company was to be called GlaxoSmithKline (GSK) and unified under a new logo. Naturally, all our templates were irrelevant. Never again, would we glimpse the trademark of SmithKlineBeecham. The logo was no more. The logo was dead.

Around the same time, we became conscious of other, similar stories. Practically every week, the effects of globalisation dominated the headlines. Takeovers, mergers, buy-outs, bankruptcy... the list went on and on. Numerous familiar visual identities had to redefine or die.

These changes were echoed in our postbox. New names and motifs appeared on bills for our mobile networks, insurance companies and energy concerns.

Even the logo on the postman had changed. Later we were to reminisce the lost logos of our youth: the manufacturer of our first game-console, the wrapper of our favourite ice-lolly, our parents' first car.

One-time precursors of our daily lives, these familiar 'landmarks' had vanished and we had hardly noticed. Yet in contrast to the ceremony and pomp that greeted their arrival, they often suffered an ignoble death. Used-up and superfluous, they were discarded or replaced by a shiny new signifier. Businesses went under, but no one shed a tear for the other loser of diversification – the logo.

Logo R.I.P. is a collection of lost design icons. Icons that despite achieving 'stylistic durability', have been deemed defunct, consigned to the logo graveyard. No longer allowed to signify.

This compilation recognises that each dead logo is a story in itself, an ideogram of its time. They are cultural barometers, expressions of a recent but bygone age. Like the sounds of an old LP or a particular smell, they transport us to what was.

Here we attempt not only to properly commemorate their demise, but also to tell their tale. The end of the book is dedicated to a series of 'obituaries'; or articles that give a short account of the logo's life, including details such as the nature of the organisation behind it and the reason for its discontinuation.

Unlike contemporary corporate identity design, many of the logos in this book weren't accompanied by lengthy press releases; their 'magic' is inherent, their ideas clear. They were designed by creatives not committees, were tested on real people like family members and directors' wives, not the clinical environment of the modern day test-group.

We bid farewell to these once familiar logos, and pay tribute both to the designer's ideas, and the corporations behind them. Join with us in mourning.

'Logo R.I.P.'

Declan and Garech Stone, The Stone Twins
Amsterdam

The term 'logotype' and its
shortened form 'logo' come
from the Greek *logos*, meaning
word. Logotype sometimes
refers to marks that are longer
and easily readable names,
while logo sometimes refers
to shorter names, acronyms or
abbreviations. Sometimes both
terms are used as synonyms for
the graphic trademark, which
also includes picture marks.

Source: Mollerup, Per, *Marks of Excellence:*
The History and Taxonomy of Trademarks,
Phaidon Press, London 1997 (P. 109)

IN MEMORIAM...

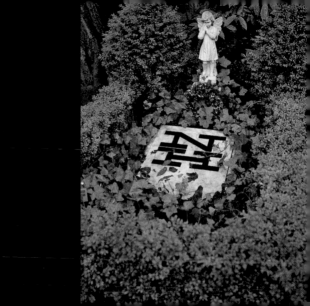

1968 – 1999

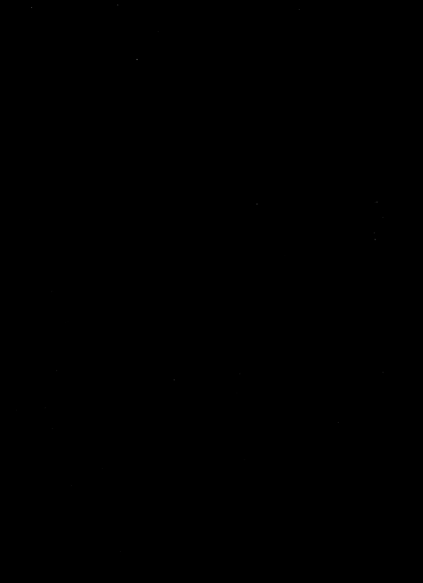

1910~2001

XVI

XVII

1975-2002

1996-2006

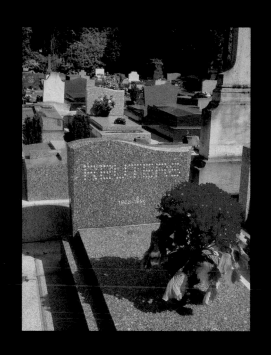

XXXVII

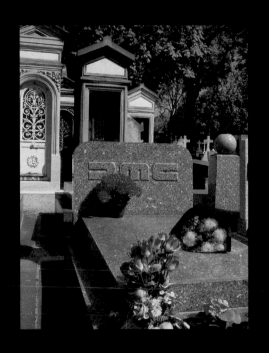

XXXIX

"… it's time for this old friend to retire with the grace and dignity it deserves. So, today, we're saying 'goodbye'…"

Mike Eskew, UPS Chairman and CEO, on the departure of Paul Rand's UPS logotype. (March 25TH, 2003)[117]

OBITUARIES

IMPERIAL AIRLINES/BOAC 'SPEEDBIRD' 1932–1984

DESIGN: THEYRE LEE-ELLIOTT (UK)

In 1932 Imperial Airlines (est. 1924) introduced a stylised motif of a bird in flight, nicknamed the 'Speedbird', as its corporate emblem. The bold logo perfectly captured the spirit of this new and exciting mode of transport. To many it is a design classic, an icon created before its time. According to designer Peter Wilbur it is a "mark which although created in an age of 100 mph aircraft is still remarkably modern in concept."[3]

The Speedbird was designed by Theyre Lee-Elliott, a noted poster artist. During the 1920s and 1930s, the artwork he produced for Imperial Airlines frequently employed this motif to illustrate the various British imperial or empire routes.

In 1939, British Overseas Airways Corporation (BOAC) was formed after the merger between Imperial Airways and British Airlines. The new state-owned national airline retained the Speedbird as its unifying symbol. By the 1950s, BOAC led many of the developments of the passenger *jet era* – and the Speedbird both evoked and expressed the glamour and romance of air travel during this period.

Throughout the 1960s, the BOAC livery of a dark blue tail with gold initials on the cheatline and a gold Speedbird on the fin was a familiar sight around the world. The Speedbird, albeit a slightly restyled version by Karl Gerstner in 1964, had survived for generations and was stylistically relevant to brand the airline even further into the future – adverts from 1971 show it visualised on the supersonic Concorde.

With the fusion of BOAC and its sister airline BEA (British European Airways) to form British Airways in 1974, the iconic Speedbird was jettisoned in favour of a truncated version of the Union Jack as the airline's logo. BA's chairman, David Nicolson, explained that the new look, by design agency Negus and Negus, expressed "a modern, efficient, confident and friendly face to the public."[4] However, after a large number of petitions from ex-BOAC staff, the Speedbird was recalled – and featured as a separate emblem on the nose section of the aircraft.[5] This diminished role for the legendary symbol lasted until 1984, when BA launched a new look, as part of its preparations for privatisation. Discarded to the dustbin of history, only the Speedbird name endures – in the title of BA's HQ and call-sign.

SWASTIKA
−1945

DESIGN: UNKNOWN

Although instantly acknowledged as the symbol of Nazi Germany, the 'Swastika' is in fact an ancient symbol. It has been found on Byzantine buildings, Buddhist inscriptions, Celtic monuments and Greek coins. Throughout the course of 3000 years it represented life, sun, power, strength and good luck.

Even in the early 20th century the Swastika, or the 'hooked cross', was a largely benign emblem used innocently as a decorative motif to signify good fortune and well being. It was frequently used on cigarette cases, postcards, coins, and buildings. During World War I, the Swastika was found on the shoulder patches of the American 45th Infantry Division and right up until the mid-1930s, Carlsberg etched it onto the base of their beer bottles.

With the rise of National Socialist Germany, Adolf Hitler decided that the NSDAP (Nationalsozialistische Deutsche Arbeiterpartei) needed its own insignia and flag. On August 7th 1920, at the Salzburg Congress, the Swastika was unveiled as the official emblem of the party. It appeared in a white circle on a crimson background. The original designer of the Nazi insignia, Dr. Friedrich Krohn (a dentist), initially drew it counter-clockwise but Hitler insisted on a change to its direction. In *Mein Kampf*, Hitler describes this reductive yet stark visual mark as the symbol "of the fight for the victory of Aryan man" and adds that it "has been and always will be anti-Semitic."[6]

From 1933, Albert Speer, Hitler's personal architect, moulded the image of Nazi Germany. He created a decorative scheme of Swastika ornamentation throughout Germany which was as pervasive as the Führer's image. To the international world, these designs broadcast the arrival of a new powerful Germany – the result of a mass will and restored national pride. Today, many regard Speer's starkly powerful designs as the beginnings of post-war corporate identity schemes.

Since the defeat of Nazi Germany by the Allies in 1945, all forms of the Swastika have been banned in many countries. Hitler took an ancient symbol and perverted it to such a degree that it can never be used again without evoking all the associations of destruction, death and vileness that the NSDAP perpetrated. If the Swastika is displayed in any part of the western world, the reactions are universally of rage and disgust.

- **BUDDHISTS + HINDUS STILL COMMONLY EMPLOY THE SWASTIKA AS A RELIGIOUS SYMBOL.**

NASA

NASA 'WORM'
1974–1992
DESIGN: DANNE & BLACKBURN (USA)

In 1975, the National Aeronautics and Space Administration (NASA), introduced a new unified visual communications system. This was commissioned as part of the US Federal Design Improvement Program, a 1972 initiative to modernise the use of design by government agencies.

A central part of the new identity was the NASA logotype, devised by Bruce Blackburn, of the New York agency Danne and Blackburn. The 'Worm', as it is more popularly known, consists of NASA's initials reduced to their simplest form, with the A's abstracted into minimal cones that metaphorically suggest rockets ready for take-off. The one width, continuous-stroke letters evoke "a feeling of unity, technological precision, thrust and orientation toward the future."[7]

The Worm was used in a vibrant shade of red, and was often accompanied by auxiliary information set in Helvetica. The logotype achieved maximum visibility during the pioneering flights of the Space Shuttle in the 1980s. According to designer Michael Johnson: "The Worm came to symbolise space travel itself – modern, flowing, sinuous, a continuous line... Corporate America identity design had its role model, and needed no further prompting... The Worm created a new benchmark to which designers could refer when they were seeking to appear 'new' and 'technological'."[8]

The emblematic design program by Danne and Blackburn, not only had to consider the design from a graphic viewpoint, but also had to take into consideration the technical aspects, such as the application of the logotype onto spacecraft, uniform patches, publications and satellite markings. Over the years, the program was widely cited, and in 1984, it was awarded one of the first Presidential Awards for Design Excellence.

In 1992, as part of a process to restore its badly shaken morale caused by the 1986 Space Shuttle disaster, NASA scrapped the clean and progressive Worm, and re-instated 'The Meatball' (an insignia comprising of a sphere, stars and orbit, designed by James Modarelli in 1959). NASA chief Daniel S. Goldin, believed that the older logo, laden with 'Buck Rogers' imagery, represented the optimistic days of glory for the space program.[9]

Nowadays, and sadly for design purists, the far superior Worm is only used on retro merchandise – a treatment viewed in some quarters as an act of cultural desecration.

P&G
'MOON AND STARS'
1882–1990s

DESIGN: UNKNOWN

In 1837, William Procter and James Gamble joined forces to form a soap company, Procter & Gamble (P&G). Originally based in Cincinnati, Ohio, today the company is regarded as one of the world's leading consumer goods conglomerates. It is the name behind a wide range of household brands, such as Pampers, Tide, Ariel and Wella.

From the 1860s, Procter & Gamble sported a logo that comprised of 13 stars to represent the original American colonies. In an era when many people could not read, the mark became a valuable identifier of P&G products. In 1882, when the trademark was officially registered with the U.S. Patent Office, a line drawing of the popular Man in the Moon motif was added. In 1932, the illustration was modified to include flowing white hair and a beard (which curled off to a point in each direction).

However, by the early 1980s, P&G started receiving complaints about the presence of satanic symbols in their enigmatic logo. Apparently, a ram can be found at the tip of the figure's beard; and a mirror image of the number 666 (or the reflected number of the beast) is inscribed by three small curls directly under his chin.

P&G publicly announced that the rumours were totally false and successfully prosecuted those responsible for spreading them – usually small rival household product manufacturers based in America's Bible Belt states. As the absurd accusations of P&G's connections to Satanism continued,[10] the company commissioned a restyle of their beleaguered trademark in 1991. This streamlined version, by Lipson Alport Glass & Associates, purged the offensive curls and ram-horns – but failed to quell the persistent stories.

According to the late Alan Fletcher: "A vivid imagination could just about conjure up a ram, but linking the stars and curls to form a mirror image of the unholy digits requires a dedicated sense of fantasy. Anyway the rumours crossed the Atlantic and slips of paper were circulated at Baptist meetings with the improbable suggestion that Satan is 'creeping into your kitchen'."[11]

In the mid-1990s, the Moon and Stars symbol was quietly sacrificed; and replaced with a neutral typographic treatment of Procter & Gamble's initials (by Peterson & Blyth). The new logo is intentionally bland and quite unlikely to stir up fantastical images. It performs better as a branded-pluralistic identity, and doesn't compete with the individual identities of P&G's products.

KODAK
'K'
1971–2006

DESIGN: PETER J. OESTREICH (USA)

Eastman Kodak was founded by businessman Henry Strong and inventor George Eastman in 1892. It is credited as the company that revolutionised photography by making the process easy to use and accessible to nearly everyone.

Eastman had a visionary mind and an intuitive grasp of marketing. Fascinated by the strong impact of the letter K, he hit upon the appellation 'Kodak' while playing anagrams with his mother. He also coined many of Kodak's early advertising slogans.[12]

Despite possessing the highly visible and inseparable insignia of red and yellow since the 1930s, the corporate signature of Kodak was rather nondescript. This all changed in 1971, when the company adopted a new unifying symbol, based on the initial letter of the corporate name. The 'K' symbol suggested a refracting lens or flash contained within a viewfinder. The striking logo was designed by

Peter J. Oestreich, a comparatively unheralded graphic designer whose studio was close to the corporate offices of Kodak in Rochester, NY.

The K exudes a powerful simplicity and was the perfect visual embodiment of Kodak's inventive, dynamic and fun personality. It formed the basis of Kodak's corporate identity system; and endured for almost 35 years. In 1987, Joseph Selame rejuvenated the logo with a typographic tweak that removed all the serifs, except for the upper one on the A and thickened the K form. He also underscored the logo with bars of diminishing thickness, that stylistically resembled the logo of the 1984 LA Olympics. This version of the logo was employed primarily to signify franchise holders or High Street retailers.

In order to survive the seismic shift from analogue to digital photography at the start of the 21st century, Kodak was forced to reinvent itself; leading to a makeover of its corporate image in 2006. The company replaced the 'K' symbol with a new streamlined wordmark, (designed by BIG, Brand Integration Group). According to Kodak, the change conveyed "the multi-industry, digital imaging leader Kodak has become".[13] It's hard to argue with that, but many in the design community were saddened to see the retirement of yet another titan of logo design.

However, the turnaround strategy failed and in January 2012, Kodak filed for bankruptcy protection – thereby raising the specter that the 132-year-old trailblazer could become the most high profile casualty of the Digital Age.

131

ENRON 'TILTED E' 1997–2001

DESIGN: PAUL RAND (USA)

Amidst much pomp and ceremony, the Enron logo – a multi-coloured tilted 'E' – was unveiled in January 1997. It signalled the beginning of an aggressive global policy by Enron (est. 1986), as it anticipated the opening of retail energy markets. Jeffrey K. Skilling, then president and CEO of Enron, declared that this was the start of "the process to take Enron from being one of the least well-known large companies, to joining McDonalds, Coca-Cola and American Express as one of the most recognised names in the world."[14]

In a brazen bid to get some instant kudos, Enron charged Paul Rand, perhaps the most influential corporate identity designer of the 20th century, with the commission. The logo, developed by Rand before his death in 1996, is a deceptively simple design and an effective mnemonic. The capital E is rich in layered ideas and associations: the bold stroke which links the 'E' and 'N' suggests pipes and cables or connectivity, whilst also representing a household plug. The three horizontal bars on the 'E' were coloured in the primary colours red, green and blue (in fact, Rand's original design used yellow instead of green, but this proved ineffective when copied or faxed).[15]

Employees of Enron quickly dubbed the logo 'the Crooked E'[16] – a reference which, even in the early days, implied more than its forty-five degree tilt. By 1997, Enron was becoming more than an energy company. It was creating new markets in water, metals, coal, paper and anything else that could be commoditised. Throughout, it had depicted itself as a highly profitable, growing company. In fact the first quarter of 2001 had put Enron on course for revenues of $240 billion – which would have made it the *Fortune No. 1* listed company.[17]

In spite of all that, in late 2001 the company's profit statements were proved to be untrue and it emerged that massive debts had been hidden. As the depth of the deception unfolded, Enron was forced to file for Chapter 11 bankruptcy. The scandal proved to be one of the biggest in corporate history and its long-term effects are likely to be felt for years to come.

Today, the Enron name is synonymous with 'corporate irresponsibility'[18] – and its infamous logo has taken on a whole new meaning. It has become the butt of stinging satire and vitriolic condemnation. According to Professor Stephen J. Eskilson, the Enron E is "the most powerful anti-logo of its time."[19]

VOC 'MONOGRAM' 1602–1799

DESIGN: UNKNOWN

The VOC, Verenigde Oost-Indische Compagnie (or the Dutch East India Company), was established in 1602 to coordinate shipping and trade with Southeast Asia. The States-General of the Netherlands gave it more than just a monopoly on trade with the Far East. It possessed quasi-governmental powers, including the ability to wage war, imprison and execute convicts, negotiate treaties, coin money and establish colonies. In this way, the "VOC was a state within the state."[20] It was also arguably one of the first mega-corporations, or multinationals – and the first company to issue stock.

In its heyday, between 1680 and 1750, the VOC had thirty trading posts in Asia. The main ones were situated on the Moluccan Islands, Ceylon and Java. During this era the VOC employed up to 50,000 people.

The graphic signature of the VOC was a distinctive monogram, incorporating the three initials: a large 'V' superimposed on the near perfect symmetry of the letters 'O' and 'C'. The design, which is devoid of any unnecessary ornamentation, is remarkably balanced, durable and aesthetically pleasing. The VOC monogram was used as a sign of legitimacy; and a signal of both authority and ownership on buildings, fortresses and factories; as well as ships, chests, glassware, chinaware, cannons, swords, muskets, pipes, publications and paper. The motif was also the central visual element on coinage from 1645; and embroidered on the white stripe of the original Dutch Tricolour of orange, white and blue.

The VOC dealt in the typical commodities such as spices, coffee, tea and tobacco, but also in more cultural items such as silks, Japanese and Chinese porcelain (inspiring the famous Delft earthenware), *objects d'art* and even elephants. By 1669, the VOC was the wealthiest private company the world had ever seen. Its riches laid the foundation for the Golden Age of the Dutch Republic (Rembrandt, Vermeer, Frans Hals, Vondel, Spinoza *et al*).

However, by the end of the 18th century, corruption, mismanagement and a decline in trade forced the VOC into bankruptcy. After 198 years of existence, the VOC was dissolved in 1799 and all its possessions were taken over by the Dutch government.[21]

Today, the elegant VOC monogram represents the glory of the company and the power of Dutch trade – whilst to others it is synonymous with bloodshed, forced trade and slavery.

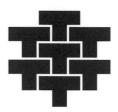

TARMAC 'SEVEN TS' 1964-1996

DESIGN: DESIGN RESEARCH UNIT (UK)

The Tarmac Company is one of the UK's foremost construction firms. Ever since its founder Edgar Purnell Hooley had accidentally discovered Tarmacadam (when he noticed that a passer-by had covered some tar spillage with waste slag),[22] the company has literally built much of Britain.

During the 1960s, there was a construction boom in the UK. Post-war prosperity created new city skylines and a motorway network extended across the country. Under the directorship of Robin Martin, Tarmac undertook a staggering expansion program. However, Tarmac's rapid growth and diversification had caused serious communication problems and confusion over the company's image.

In 1963, Design Research Unit (DRU) – one of the first generation of British design consultancies combining expertise in architecture, graphics and industrial design – was commissioned to design a new symbol to represent the new concern. Designer Ronald Armstrong created a strikingly bold solution, that was contemporary in spirit and progressive in outlook. Dubbed the 'Seven Ts', the symbol communicates myriad meanings: the seven merged companies, construction and the 'T' for tarmac. As DRU explained: "The scheme was designed for eventual extension to all the companies in the group, a unification which is expressed in the symbolic cluster of seven Ts."[23]

The symbol became an ever-present icon in the British landscape during the rapid motorway expansion in the 1960s and 1970s (throughout this period, the Tarmac logo was often an unwelcome sight as it was synonymous with delays due to roadworks). By 1974, Tarmac's logo was "voted one of the world's top trademarks."[24]

As Tarmac diversified further in the 1970s, going into house building and property development, it became a worldwide player. In the 1980s it was one of the lead companies involved in the construction of the Channel Tunnel. Nevertheless, by the late 1980s, high interest rates caused serious problems. After recording record losses in 1992, the company fragmented and refocused on its three core activities: quarry products, housing and construction.

On May 1st 1996, Tarmac unveiled a new corporate identity (designed by Enterprise IG) to represent this change in strategy: a single green and white T on an oval yellow background. After more than 30 years service, the famous 'Seven Ts' logo was discontinued.

THE NEW HAVEN
RAILROAD 'NH'
1954–1968

DESIGN: HERBERT MATTER (USA)

The New York, New Haven and Hartford Railroad Company, commonly known as the New Haven Railroad, operated in the states of Connecticut, New York, Rhode Island and Massachusetts from 1872 to 1968. The company operated freight and passenger trains over a Boston – New York City main line and a number of branch lines. In its heyday, the New Haven was generally considered the largest and most important transportation enterprise in New England.

With the arrival of new president Patrick McGinnis in 1954, Herbert Matter, the Swiss émigré designer and poster artist, was commissioned to create a corporate identity for the railroad. In line with many other large American Corporations (e.g. IBM and Westinghouse) The New Haven was endowed with an international Modernist aesthetic. Matter replaced the railroad's unfocused and highly ornate script wordmark (which had existed since 1891) with an eloquent logo composed of its initials 'NH'. The stacked elongated slab serif letterforms aptly evoke a rail-network, connection-points or rail tracks. Over the next two years, Matter and his associate Norman Ives moulded a comprehensive visual identity for New Haven – a prodigious amount covering brochures, adverts, timetables and the famous train livery of black, red and white.

As with most of Matter's work, the NH logo is as compelling now as it was back in the 1950s. The great Paul Rand, when celebrating Matter's oeuvre, once said: "His work of '32 could have been done in '72 or even '82. It has that timeless, unerring quality one recognises instinctively. It speaks to all tongues, with one tongue. It is uncomplicated, to the point, familiar, and yet unexpected."[25]

However, by 1960, the New Haven Railroad was approaching insolvency and the company filed for bankruptcy a year later. After a decade of struggling along under various trustees, the New Haven Railroad was absorbed by the ill-fated Penn Central Transportation Company in 1968. The NH symbol, which had become one of the most identifiable symbols in America, had hit the buffers.

In a strange twist of fate, the classic NH logo was revived, and lives on as heritage livery for a different railroad company, the New Haven line of MetroNorth Commuter Railroad (MNCRR).

135

BRITISH STEEL 'S'
1969–1999
DESIGN: DAVID GENTLEMAN (UK)

British Steel was a major UK steel producer established under the Iron and Steel Act of 1967 – a decree that brought together 90% of Britain's steelmaking companies.

In 1969, David Gentleman (an artist-designer who is perhaps better known for his illustration, stamp design, protest graphics and wood engravings, in an impressive career spanning nearly six decades) was commissioned to design a symbol for the newly nationalised corporation. Gentleman was only approached after another design firm's work was rejected by the client. As a one-man practice, and working to an extremely tight time-frame, he devised a logo masterpiece.[26]

Whilst gaining insights into the steelmaking process, Gentleman became fascinated by iron samples that were contorted for strength and stress tests. These incidental shapes inspired a symbol consisting of two bent steel plates that formed the letter 'S'.

According to Gentleman, the idea "came first from my own wish to suggest that steel was strong and flexible. Only later did I discover that steel was bent in order to test its strength ... so I used this as a rationale, but I didn't know that at the time!"[27]

The simple geometry of the customised 'S', which shares the same proportions as the A series of international paper sizes, meant it could easily reproduce at any scale. Apart from black or white, the symbol could only be rendered in Pacific Blue. It was used in many iterations, from huge steel plants to print collateral and livery assets such as trucks and trains.

The motif is a harmonious marriage between form and content – and expressed the characteristics of a powerful industrial process with great economy. According to designer Mike Dempsey, Gentleman's symbol is "the epitome of pure modernist graphic design," – "maximum effect employing the minimum of elements. It is witty, distinctive, memorable and over four decades on, it still looks fresh and beautiful."[28]

Gentleman's design survived both a conversion of the company as a public limited company (PLC) and privatisation in 1988. However by 1999, British Steel had agreed to amalgamate with Hoogovens of the Netherlands. As 'a merger of equals', the new concern adopted a new name Corus and logo (designed by Enterprise IG). British Steel's unforgettable symbol was deemed obsolete and ungraciously dumped on the scrapheap.

ROBERTSON'S 'GOLLY'
1910—2001
DESIGN: UNKNOWN (UK)

Robertson's was one of the most popular producers of jam and marmalade in Britain. To many, the brand is still synonymous with the cartoon figure of 'Golly'. With his natty bow tie and trousers, flowing jacket and distinctive yellow waistcoat, Golly danced his way across the labels of Robertson's products for 91 years. He was a living versatile mascot-like logo.

According to official records, John Robertson (the son of the founder) was so intrigued by the popularity of the Golly doll on a visit to the US, that he thought it would make an ideal mascot for the company. In 1910, the character was registered as a trade mark. In 1928, Robertson's introduced the first of their enamelled badges, a Golly golfer. For the next 60 years, Golly was depicted in numerous guises and the badges became highly sought after collectibles.

However, by the 1980s, fictional characters such as Golly, *Little Black Sambo* and the Dutch *Zwarte Piet* were regularly caught in the eye of politically correct storms. Groups campaigning for racial equality found Robertson's beloved mascot offensive. They pointed to Golly's origins as a 'Golliwog' (a caricature of black-faced minstrels) and to the association with the word 'wog', a racial epithet comparable to 'nigger'. They claimed he was an unpleasant stereotype from another time who had somehow survived against the odds into a multicultural age.

In contrast, others deemed Golly an innocent grinning character who brightened the breakfast tables and jam sandwiches of millions of children. The late, great designer Alan Fletcher once observed: "What is currently termed 'politically correct', could on occasion be rephrased 'morally enfeebled'. What's so offensive about golliwogs? They are a jolly caricature and no more racially offensive than a podgy John Bull or a spindly Uncle Sam."[29]

Robertson's defended Golly as a fictional nurseryland character, not a depiction of a black person. In the late-1980s, the company came under increasing pressure and moved Golly to the back of jam jars, and removed it from TV adverts. Finally in 2001, the company bowed to the inevitable, and shelved their contentious mascot. Brand director Ginny Knox said: "While we are obviously sad to say farewell to Golly, like any successful brand we're constantly evolving to ensure that we remain interesting to today's consumers... We are not bowing to political correctness, but like with any great brand we have to move with the times."[30]

137

ENERGIE NOORD WEST 'JUPITER' 1996–1999

DESIGN: BRS PREMSELA VONK (NL)

Traditionally, Dutch energy companies were mostly municipally-owned and provincial multi-utilities covering gas, electricity, water and waste. The opening of energy markets in the 1990s meant that for the first time, they were exposed to competition from neighbouring countries. In response to this, the Dutch companies consolidated through a series of mergers, and some alliances with multinationals. In 1996, Energie Noord West (ENW) was formed after a merger between five energy companies from the north-west of the Netherlands.

To represent this new company, design agency BRS Premsela Vonk (now called Edenspiekermann) was commissioned to create a new image – one which would help position ENW as a powerful and dynamic energy company.

The design-team developed a motif based on the Roman god Jupiter.

This mythological figure, who was king of the gods and ruler of the universe, is an appropriate visual metaphor for an energy company. Jupiter was originally the god of the sky and of such atmospheric phenomena as thunder and lightning. He used a thunderbolt as a weapon and had the power to send the earth clear weather, rain or destructive storms.

According to official BRS literature, the motif shows Jupiter distributing energy via a thunderbolt. They add that it was a conscious decision to choose a classical symbol because "it is timeless and durable, allowing continuity of the corporate identity for a longer period."[31] Over several months, this dynamic motif was applied to the company's vast fleet of vehicles, staff uniforms, company properties and stationery.

ENW's Jupiter can be seen as part of a wider trend for anthropomorphic images that had invaded the corporate identity landscape ten years earlier. The Prudential 'Dame', the BT 'Piper', Akzo's 'Bruce' and the Rabobank 'Man on Sundial' were all conspicuous strategies to project a more friendly corporate image.

In February 1999, ENW merged with three other Dutch energy companies to form NUON ENW; as part of a continued strategy towards becoming a pan-European force. Despite its beauty and graphic strength, never mind the exorbitant implementation costs, Jupiter disappeared in a puff of smoke and was replaced by the purple and lime livery of NUON (designed by Tel Design).

RILEY
'DIAMOND BADGE'
1919–1969
DESIGN: HARRY RUSH (UK)

Riley is one of many long-gone car marques. Together with Austin-Healey, Hillman, Humber, Jensen, Morris, Rover, Triumph, Wolseley and countless others, it is part of a proud British automotive history *(see 'Rover' page 167)*.

The Riley Company was founded by William Riley in 1896. The original Rileys were motorised tricycles that developed into automobiles as their design progressed. In 1919, the Diamond Badge appeared for the first time on the '11HP'. The car's designer and accomplished draughtsman, Harry Rush, probably developed the stylised Riley script: a handwritten signature that signals pride, quality and craftsmanship. The design is typical of a period when most companies used the founder's signature as a guarantee of authenticity: e.g. Kellogg's, Ford and AEG; and remained virtually intact for half a century. From 1921, the badge was often accompanied by the slogan

"As old as the industry, as modern as the hour."

Throughout the 1920s and 1930s, Riley grew in fame with a collection of impressive saloons and fine sports cars. During this era they dominated many racetracks and rallies. To the public, their cars were noted for their individual and elegant designs – of which there were many varieties. According to one advert "we make far too many models of course. But then we have a pretty fertile design department, and we like making nice, interesting cars."[32]

In the 1950s and 1960s, the entire British motor industry went through massive consolidation. For many companies, mergers and take-overs became the only route to survival. The result was a metamorphosis from relatively small, individually run businesses, to large conglomerates such as the British Motor Corporation (BMC). By 1955 no more thoroughbred Rileys were built. Enthusiasts lament this period, when many famous British automotive brands were slowly debased on a series of *badge-engineered* BMC saloons. After the formation of British Leyland in 1968, several proud marques were discontinued. In July 1969, the last radiator grille adorned with the Riley Diamond Badge rolled off the production line: the Kestrel 1300 MK II.

Today, the Riley trademark is owned by BMW. As with once-defunct, yet glamorous and heritage-rich British brands, (such as Mini and MG), it is possible that the Riley badge could be resurrected in the future.

3M
'PLUMBER'S GOTHIC'
1961–1977

DESIGN: GERALD STAHL & ASSOC. (USA)

Founded in 1902, the 3M Company (originally the Minnesota Mining and Manufacturing Co.) is a diversified manufacturer of innovative commercial and consumer products – ranging from everyday items such as Scotch Tape and Post-it notes, to industrial abrasives and construction materials.

By 1960, the continued growth and diversification of its operations had adversely affected corporate unity. To solve this identity crisis, 3M commissioned Gerald Stahl & Associates to create a definitive logo that would unite the corporation and all its business units under a single sign. The result was a logotype composed of two identical forms: a numeral '3' and letter 'M' in slab serif letterforms. The trademark formed a solid base rectangle which reflected the strength and stability of the company.

When the new logo was unveiled in 1961, Joseph C. Duke, 3M executive vice president, explained: "When one product division or subsidiary makes a favourable impression anywhere, every other 3M division, subsidiary or product should benefit. In turn, the achievements and prestige of the 3M company should benefit each product and activity of the company."[33]

The new graphic system also included a proprietary typeface – dubbed as 'Plumber's Gothic' – which maintained the same character established by the trademark.

In 1965, Brooks Stevens Associates was hired to fine-tune the identification program and look after packaging (which was specifically excluded from the 1961 system). The firm's concept called for each 3M package to have three colour blocks: the first identifying the product, the second identifying the division and the third carrying the 3M logo, as developed earlier by Stahl.[34] The design program, which became known as the 'Mondriaan scheme' (due to the geometric patterns), proved to be full of vitality and character and ensured unity and recognition of the 3M brand.

However, by the 1970s, the visual identity, although stunning and individually brilliant in parts, was considered to be outdated and ineffective for a company boasting the latest technological advances. In 1977, 3M adopted a new identity created by Siegel+Gale. Driven by their *Simple is Smart* philosophy,[35] was a new logo: an undemanding symbol consisting of the '3' and 'M' juxtaposed and set in extra-bold sans-serif letterforms.

MAC FISHERIES
'ST. ANDREW'S CROSS'
1952–1968

DESIGN: HANS SCHLEGER (UK)

In 1919, the wealthy industrialist and founder of the Lever Brothers empire, Lord Leverhulme, established Mac Fisheries. The company pioneered commercial fishing techniques – and established a chain of fish mongers throughout Britain.

For nearly fifty years, 'Mac Fish', as it was more popularly known, was as ubiquitous as McDonalds is today. At its height in the 1950s, there were over 400 branches.

In 1952, the legendary designer Hans Schleger, known by his pseudonym Zéró, was commissioned by advertising agency Mather & Crowther to create a new corporate identity for Mac Fisheries. Schleger started with a redesign of their old symbol – a circular mark that incorporated the St. Andrew's diagonal cross from the Scottish flag with four icons of fish swimming west – making it more robust, streamlined and modern.

He then implemented a modular identification system for packaging, where the quadrants of the symbol were colour-coded to represent different product lines. In advertising, Schleger introduced illustrations combined with a simple handwriting style, that differed each time. This idea reflected the fishmongers' tradition of chalking up a day's catch on a blackboard, to convey a feeling of freshness. Over the years, the solution proved a corporate image could be recognisable and personal without being fixed and rigid. It appeared free, yet was disciplined. In addition, it was a pioneering holistic approach to an advertising campaign.

Ken Garland, design luminary, spoke admirably of Schleger's work for Mac Fisheries when he said: "There have been many more ambitious, more compendious – and, some would say, more grandiose – corporate identity schemes than this in the last 30 years; but none, I think, more sympathetic, more inventive or more endearing,"[36]

In the 1960s, there was a dramatic shift away from fresh fish consumption. Reflecting this change and in a bid to offer a broader brand offering, Mac Fish rebranded as Mac Market in 1968. Schleger's logo underwent a dramatic makeover, with the four fish losing their heads and fins to leave a quartet of abstract ovals. In strategic terms, the change was logical – yet the company was unable to compete with other grocery retailers that had eroded its market share. In 1979, the last Mac Market shops were closed for good.

XEROX
'DIGITAL X'
1994–2008

DESIGN: LANDOR ASSOCIATES (USA)

The Haloid Photographic Company, a manufacturer of photographic paper and equipment was founded in 1906 in Rochester, NY. From 1961, the company was simply known as Xerox, in recognition of the success of one its innovative products: a plain paper photocopier using the process of xerography. As it expanded to become a leader in office technologies, the brand name 'Xerox' virtually became synonymous with photocopying.[37]

By the early 1990s, Xerox sought to turn its products into a service, providing a complete document service to companies including supply, maintenance and support. In 1994, to reinforce this strategy, the company introduced a prominent corporate signature *The Document Company* above its main logo (the restrained symmetrical wordmark devised by Chermayeff & Geismar in 1968) and a new corporate symbol: a red 'Digital X'. With an ascending arm dissipating into pixels, the trademark was conceived to signal the increasing movement of documents between the analog and digital worlds. Designed by Margo Zucker of Landor Associates, the Digital X was distinctive, communicative and expressive of the place that Xerox occupied at that moment – bridging new and old technologies and processes. The design was an inventive interpretation of a conspicuous letter; and recognition of X as the quintessential mark. The immediacy and vigour of the symbol (together with tremendous advertising resources) quickly established it in the public mind.

By the first decade of the 21st century, Xerox faced new challenges and decided to revamp its image as a software and technology service provider. In January 2008, the company announced that it would retire the Digital X in favour of "a brand identity that reflects the Xerox of today."[38] The new logo consists of a lower-case 'xerox' that sits alongside a red sphere sketched with lines that link to form a stylised X (designed by Interbrand). According to the company, the new symbol represents "Xerox's connections to its customers, partners, industry and to innovation."[39]

The successor of the Digital X is formally less distinguished, and joins the recent epidemic of Digital Age clichés, such as shaded spheres and bubblified forms (e.g. AT&T, GSK and KPN). This is a sad trend in corporate identity design that is fuelled by the latest software, and mired in its own spin of meaning.

TELECOM ÉIREANN
'TE'
1983–1999
DESIGN: KDW (IRL)

Throughout the 1990s, many national telephone companies decided to change their corporate identity in order to meet the challenges of a deregulated market-place. In the process, many design icons were lost. One such example was the logo of Telecom Éireann (TE), the national telephone company of Ireland.

Telecom Éireann was established in 1983 after the division of the Department of Posts and Telegraphs into two independent entities. The company's trademark was designed by Peter Dabinett of Kilkenny Design Workshops (KDW), which was the world's first state-sponsored design agency from 1963–1988. The logo combines the traditional Irish uncial forms of 'T' and 'E' in a modern graphic simplicity. The joined initials neatly suggest several relevant ideas, as in a telephone dial, handset or coiled cable. In the motif, international style

converges with the spiral ornamentation characteristic of pre-Christian Ireland, to convey a modern semi-state company proud of its local heritage.[40]

For nearly 16 years, the 'Snail', as the TE logo was nicknamed, appeared on public phone-boxes, vehicle liveries, signage, uniforms, stationery, call-cards and the daily televised weather reports.

Nevertheless, an Irish government review (from 1998), had shown that, given changes in technology, competition through liberalisation and ownership changes, the range of services provided by Telecom Éireann went far beyond straightforward telephony. What was needed, according to the study, was a brand that accommodated all aspects of the business. The review also showed that Telecom Éireann was a company which was monopolistic, not particularly friendly, and had a 'nine-to-five' culture.[41]

In 1999, the company was rebranded as Eircom, with a new logo composed of a stylised orange globe (developed by the Identity Business). Many in the design community united in grief for Dabinett's masterpiece and were highly critical of the adoption of yet another ubiquitous 'swoosh-ball' – a brandmark that only expresses the homogeneity of globalisation. Unlike the Telecom Éireann logo, Eircom's globe is a bland, uniform design isolated from the particulars of Irish visual culture. The rebrand was also viewed as a missed opportunity, as traditionally the image of a country's telephone or postal company is the most powerful expression of its design.

143

CCA 'BOX'
1957–1986

DESIGN: RALPH ECKERSTROM (USA)

The Container Corporation of America (CCA) was a specialist manufacturer of paperboard and paper-based packaging. The company was founded by Walter Paepcke in 1926. Although a tough-minded businessman with an unswerving eye for the bottom line, Paepcke believed his business would flourish if the world around him did. Such visionary notions helped forge CCA into one of the most admired corporations in America.

Paepcke's ideals and values found resonance with the European emigrés who had fled the evils of Nazi Germany. Design luminaries such as Egbert Jacobson, Herbert Bayer, Ralph E. Eckerstrom and John Massey were all successive design directors of CCA. Well before it was common practice, design was made an organic component of the corporate culture of CCA.

In 1957, Eckerstrom, who headed CCA's design department at the time, brought to his job the tenets of the new Swiss design movement – that emphasised cleanliness, readability and objectivity. He replaced the cluttered old logo of CCA (an illustration of a cardboard box, centred on an outline of the US, designed by Egbert Jacobson) with a much simpler and progressive design. Eckerstrom's logo consisted of the three corporate initials in a rectangle, with two corners sheared at a forty-five degree angle to imply an isometric box. The logo has an unassuming, effortless and lucid quality which instantly conveys CCA as belonging to the 'box business'. For nearly thirty years, the CCA logo was the cornerstone of a unique corporate design history – and is regularly touted as one of the 20th century's finest and most memorable trademarks.

The advertising campaign *Great Ideas of Western Man* was the perfect embodiment of Paepcke's philosophy. The print ads aspired to propagate the important concepts of western civilisation – a noble notion for a company that simply made boxes. The campaign was to become one of the most famous in history, running for 25 years. Although he had dismissed it at first, the late David Ogilvy, advertising legend and guru, later admitted that it was "one of the best corporate campaigns that has ever appeared."[42]

When CCA was bought by Mobil Oil in 1978, the entire corporate communications department was laid to rest. By 1986, another takeover by Jefferson Smurfit spelt the end of the classic CCA logo. In 1998, the CCA brand name was completely phased out.

PHARMACIA & UPJOHN 'THE HAND, BIRD, STAR' 1996–2000

DESIGN: NEWELL AND SORRELL (NL)

In the late 1990s, the pharmaceutical industry was the dominant force in the colossal consolidation trends. Corporate histories and their trademarks were subject to revision and disappearance when mergers, acquisitions and rebranding of companies at best led to a truncation of the past, and at worst to an erasure.

One short-lived corporate entity was Pharmacia & Upjohn, a product of a merger of equals between two historic drug companies Pharmacia of Sweden and The Upjohn Company of North America in 1995. It created, at the time, one of the largest pharmaceutical groups in Europe – a conglomerate with combined sales of around £4.5 billion.[43]

In February 1996, a new visual identity was launched to signal the birth of the new concern. The logo featured part of a purple rock face with three symbols inspired by prehistoric cave drawings. Titled 'the Hand, Bird, Star', the symbol, which can be described as both a figurative and narrative logo, was designed by the Amsterdam branch of Newell and Sorrell (now Interbrand). Tony Allen, managing director, explained: "The new identity was created to express an idea about humanity, strength, compassion and aspiration."[44] He suggested that the identity of Pharmacia & Upjohn transcended language barriers and appealed to a global audience, one which would recognise such symbols and be able to translate them, with little question of misinterpretation.

Design experts hailed the program enthusiastically. They saw it as a more consumer-friendly and humanistic design approach that contrasted with the cold monolithic look endemic to the world of pharma identity design. Nevertheless, it was not short of critics. Traditionalists envisioned reproduction problems, whilst the Upjohn contingent dubbed the logo "the Upjohn tombstone"[45] and saw it as a symbol of a troubled merger and a clash of cultures.

However, the eye-catching logo was short-lived. In 2000, Pharmacia & Upjohn agreed a merger with Monsanto, an American biotech company, to form a new $50 billion corporation Pharmacia.[46] Along with the heritage brand name of Upjohn, the 'purple rock' logo was also dropped. The new concern deliberately chose a conservative wordmark – a polar opposite of the creativity of its predecessor.

145

'MEXICO 68'
1965–1968

DESIGN: EDUARDO TERRAZAS (MEX)
LANCE WYMAN (USA)

The Mexico Olympics were the first Olympics held in Latin America. They are remembered for many things: Mexico City's high-altitude, student riots, Beamon's spectacular long jump and a Black Panther salute. The XIX Olympiad is also noted as a milestone in the evolution of graphic systems.

Led by architect Pedro Ramírez Vázquez, the design program, in particular the wayfinding scheme, married rigorous pragmatism with a visual fiesta. Central to the graphic system was the 'Mexico 68' logotype. The form is a clever integration of the five Olympic rings and the number '68'. The original sketches for the logo were done as a series of *tablas* by a group of Huichol artists. Central to their visual language is the use of convergent, parallel and concentric lines. Eduardo Terrazas then developed a lineal typographic font. Further refinement and the implementation of the concept was realised by Lance Wyman. An important kinetic application of the logotype was created by radiating its parallel lines outward to form a pattern of infinite size. On pavilions, posters and other advertising material, the resulting patterns created dazzling and eye-catching visual effects.[47]

The Mexico 68 logotype is simply a design masterpiece. It reveals the combined influences of international style, the patterns of the Huichol Indians and Op Art (which was then the preeminent artistic movement). Importantly, the overall image powerfully expressed a sense of place and culture. It was the perfect visual embodiment for the aspirations of Mexico, then an emerging Third World nation, "as a modern, current, contemporary country."[48] The design was not just branding an Olympiad but an entire nation. According to Vázquez: "We wanted the whole world to remember the event and through the event to remember Mexico."[49]

The Mexico 68 logotype is perhaps the last great Olympic trademark which was not shamelessly exploited. Although the games are floated on a tide of high-minded idealism, they are now supported by aggressive marketing campaigns and licensing deals – that sell the right to 'exploit' the logo to the highest bidder.

Soon after the XIX Olympiad, the Mexico 68 logo was officially retired. Similar to the branding devices of other major global events (e.g. World Cups, Expos) and unique amongst design solutions, the expiry date is clearly stated *(see 'Festival of Britain' page 164)*.

NeXT 'CUBE'
1986–1996

DESIGN: PAUL RAND (USA)

NeXT, Inc. was a short-lived computer company, known to the public for its series of futuristic computers and to the programming world for its operating system.

NeXT was founded in 1985 by Steve Jobs after he resigned from Apple in the same year. Three years later, its first product the *NeXT Computer*, was unveiled. It was dubbed 'The Cube' because of its sleek black magnesium case, which measured one foot on all sides. It was a watershed moment in workstation design – for the first time, the look of the computer was just as important as its speed or specific technical capabilities.

With typical flamboyance, Steve Jobs sought special dispensation from IBM to have the same logo designer for his new company: Paul Rand. Explaining the decision to pay Rand $100,000 for the mark he said: "Paul understood the purpose and power of logos better than anyone in history – he was also

the greatest living graphic designer."[50] Despite the exorbitant fee, Rand refused to produce any design options. According to Jobs, Rand said "I will solve your problem for you and you will pay me. You don't have to use the solution. If you want options, go talk to other people."[51]

Rand developed a distinctive logo that framed the word 'Next' in a black cube to evoke Jobs' proposed computer. He made the letter 'e' lowercase as a mnemonic factor; and explained that it could stand for "education, excellence, expertise, $E=mc^2$, etc..."[52] The brightly coloured letters (vermilion, yellow, green and cerise) combined with the skewed box conveyed a playful, lively logo – brimming with informality, yet authority. According to Rand "What is essential is finding a meaningful device, some idea – preferably product related – that reinforces the company name. The cube, in which the computer will be housed, can be such a device because it has visual impact, and is easy to remember."[53] The NeXT logo is another example of Rand's genius which was characterised by simplicity, wit and a rational approach to problem solving (*see 'Enron' page 132 and 'UPS' page 174*).

However, the NeXT machines were plagued by problems and sold slowly. In 1993, NeXT dropped its hardware line, but continued to sell the operating system. Three years later, NeXT was acquired by Apple. The deal brought Jobs back to the company he co-founded, and forced NeXT into one final shutdown.

RUC 'HARP & CROWN'

1922–2001

DESIGN: UNKNOWN

The Royal Ulster Constabulary (RUC) was the name of the police force in Northern Ireland from 1922 to 2001. For much of this time, it was one of the most controversial policing operations in the UK. Uniquely, the RUC had a dual role, of providing a normal law enforcement service while protecting Northern Ireland from the terrorist activities of outlawed groups.

Throughout thirty years of the Troubles (a period of ethnopolitical conflict in Northern Ireland, conventionally dated from the late 1960s to 1998), the RUC was in the front-line fighting terrorism. More than 300 of its officers tragically lost their lives and upwards of 10,000 were maimed.[54]

Unfortunately, the RUC did not enjoy unanimous support. Nationalists continually accused the force of one-sided policing and discrimination. They viewed it with much suspicion because of the fact that the majority of its members were Protestant.

In 1999, a report published by The Independent Commission on Policing (set up under the Good Friday Peace Agreement), recommended that the RUC be renamed and that its cap badge be replaced in order to foster cross-community confidence. The chairman, Chris Patten, said that its key objective was to "depoliticise" policing.[55]

The contentious emblem of the RUC was an elaborate, almost esoteric, design. Ironically, some viewed it as ideal in representing an inclusive police force in Northern Ireland – as the insignia featured symbols, or heraldic elements, from both traditions: a Royal crown (Unionist) and the shamrock and harp of Brian Boru (Nationalist). Nevertheless, a new name and badge were still necessary in order to inspire trust and confidence amongst Nationalists. In a land where symbols traditionally promote division rather than mutual respect, the process of designing the badge was a highly emotive and protracted affair.

In 2001, the RUC was rebranded as the Police Service of Northern Ireland (PSNI). The form of the new badge is an eight-pointed star (the standard insignia of the police forces of Great Britain), that incorporates a red St. Patrick's saltire and a mélange of symbols. These symbols allude to both sides of the sectarian divide (crown, harp, shamrock) and represent reconciliation (a scales of justice, torch and laurel leaf). In essence, the new logo makes a statement of compromise, in the hope for a peaceful and inclusive Northern Ireland.

TRANSAMERICA 'T'
1967–1989

DESIGN: SANDGREN & MURTHA (USA)

Transamerica Corporation was founded by A.P. Giannini in 1928, with the idea that he would invest in and serve the often overlooked small businesses and farmers in his community. By the 1960s, Transamerica had ballooned into a $12 billion conglomerate with diverse interests in air travel, entertainment, insurance, finance, manufacturing and transportation.[56]

For many years, Transamerica followed a brand-dominant approach in which the relationships between the subsidiaries and the parent were de-emphasised. In the late 1960s, company executives decided to take advantage of the synergies that a unified corporate identity could render. As part of the implementation program, Transamerica adopted the 'T' logo as a unifying symbol to connect its vast business empire.[57]

The flowing, bifurcated T symbol was created by Don Ervin, whilst at the design partnership of Sandgren &

Murtha. Ervin is regarded as a prolific and unheralded graphic designer who played an integral role in shaping the image of corporate America. In fact, his logos, for some of America's biggest companies such as Conoco, Cargill and MetLife *(see page 155)*, are better known than the man himself.[58]

With the Transamerica T, Ervin displayed the modernist philosophy of less is more; devising a form that is both elegant and evocative. The logo communicates myriad meanings (such as bold, dynamic, expansive growth) and was a highly effective encapsulation of Transamerica's multifaceted holdings. Although Ervin let his work speak for itself, he did write a notable manifesto that outlined excellence in logo design. The Transamerica T ticks much of this criteria, that lists amongst others: "It should be simple enough to be memorable. It should be long lasting and not out of date ten years from now."[58]

Outside the United States, the T symbol was best known as the emblem of United Artists film studio. Many classic films – such as *Apocalypse Now*, *Rocky*, *One Flew Over the Cuckoo's Nest* and *Carrie* – were introduced with an animated version of the logo, and the tagline "Entertainment from the Transamerica Corporation."

In 1989, Transamerica adopted a new logo: a stylised illustration of its iconic San Francisco headquarters, a sleek white pyramid. The rebrand signalled its metamorphosis from a fully diversified global conglomerate to a business specialising in insurance and other financial services.

149

BETAMAX 'β'
1975–2002
DESIGN: SONY DESIGN CENTRE (JP)

In 1975, the Betamax video format was launched by Sony, under the slogan *time shift* – which encapsulated the revolution that was about to take place in global TV habits. For the first time, viewers were freed from the constraints of watching television programmes on the day they were broadcast.

According to Sony, the name Beta is derived from the Japanese word used to describe the recording system. The symbol was originally a variation of their U-Matic logo. In 1979, the design was streamlined to look like the Greek letter 'β' – whilst also resembling a spool of tape in the loading system. In addition, the symbol "is associated with good luck and can be construed as a drawn out pronunciation of the English word 'better'. Max, an abbreviation of the word maximum, was intended to impart a meaning of grandness, and was then added to the end."[59]

The Betamax β belongs to the vast category of minuscule symbols and logos that adorn the casing of any electrical device and its peripherals. These graphical symbols act as a visual shorthand for device compatibility and a common technological language. They are usually owned by the International Electrotechnical Commission (IEC), an international standards organisation for all 'electrotechnology'.

As Betamax quickly became the first commercially successful home videotape format, Sony expected other manufacturers to back it. However, they were dealt a shock when JVC released their own *VHS* format, and Philips-Grundig developed a third format, the *Video 2000*. Over the next decade, a bitter commercial and marketing battle, dubbed 'the Format War', was played out between the rival manufacturers.

Unlike JVC, Sony refused to share its technology with other companies and by 1987, the position of VHS was unassailable. With a 95% share of the market, *Rolling Stone* magazine declared that 'the battle is over.'[60] By the end of the year, Sony produced a line of VHS video recorders.

Despite the retreat, Sony continued producing Beta recorders, and held on for years as a niche product. In 2002, Sony finally announced it would be discontinuing Betamax products.[61] Rapid sales growth in DVD players had posed a threat in recent years not just to the remnants of Betamax but to the mainstream VHS recorders. The Betamax β joined the long list of obsolete technology and IEC symbols. After all, the future was digital.

SPRATT'S 'DOG'
1936–1972
DESIGN: MAX FIELD-BUSH (UK)

Spratt's Patent Ltd. was founded by James Spratt of Cincinnati, Ohio, just before the turn of the 20th century. Spratt had originally travelled to London to sell lightening conductors but after watching half-starved dogs eating discarded crackers on the quayside, he turned his attention to producing biscuits especially for dogs. The company launched the first commercially manufactured pet food circa 1860: Spratt's' 'Meat Fibrine Dog Cakes' – a baked mixture of wheat, beet root and vegetables bound together with beef blood.

Spratt largely owed his success to the fact that he was a pioneer in mass marketing techniques, in terms of advertising and branding. Spratt's cakes were touted as a superior way of feeding pets, and came in a tin decorated with the tagline "My Faithful Friend's Own Biscuit Box". Adverts claimed they were "the backbone of the Canine Race – are the staple food for

all adult dogs." In fact, Spratt's was the first company to utilise multi-coloured billboards in London.

In the 1930s, the Spratt's company diversified into many other types and varieties of pet food. These products were all branded with a series of 'calligrams' – a graphic device that combines thought, letters and picture. Each trademark featured either a 'Scottish Terrier' dog, fish, canary bird or cat; and almost magically, the typographic forms spelt Spratt's. The logotypes were an instant success and have a character, wit and graphic strength that is rarely seen today. Paradoxically, the designs are naive yet sophisticated – and unique in logo-world, they make one smile. According to Geoff Halpin (of Identica): "It was the first marque I remember seeing as a child and has been a profound influence on me as a graphic designer. Although designed in the 1930s, it still looks fresh today."[62]

In the 1950s, as the pet food market became increasingly more sophisticated, Spratt's caught the eye of global industrial giants looking to diversify. Spratt's was first acquired by General Mills; and then, in the early 1960s, the entire business was hived off to a subsidiary, Spillers Dog Foods.

Despite pioneering the development of commercial pet food, Spratt's failed to retain their unique visual identity. The amiable logotypes were soon erased by the slick sameness of globalisation. In 1972, the Spratt's brand was replaced by Spillers and the charming calligrams were canned forever.

LUCENT 'INNOVATION RING' 1996–2006

DESIGN: LANDOR ASSOCIATES (USA)

When AT&T was forced to split into three divisions in 1996, it created a $21 billion systems and technology company without an identity or a name. Landor Associates was challenged to devise both. Remarkably, over a highly accelerated time-frame of 12 weeks from the project kick-off meeting to official management approval, Landor managed to develop one of the most daring corporate trademarks in recent history.[63]

According to Landor's rhetoric, the name Lucent means "glowing light"; and was chosen as it "expressed the energy, innovation, entrepreneurial spirit, and clear vision of the company's purpose, principles, and future".[64] Reinforcing the sense of differentiation in the crowded telecommunications industry, the logo (created by Henrik Olsen) was a red circle rendered in a single bold brush stroke. "The hand-drawn simplicity evinces and reinforces the personal, emotional appeal of human communication enabled by technology".[65] Officially named the 'Innovation Ring', the logo broke the mould. In contrast to the hard-edged geometric marks to the world of corporate identity design, the symbol appeared so casual and informal.

But, the unorthodox design of the Innovation Ring was widely derided, and prompted much hilarity amongst the media and countless desktop design critics. It was nicknamed "a big red zero" and "the Coffee Ring of Excellence."[66] Others protested that it was a crass commercialisation of the ensō, a Zen Buddhist symbol for absolute enlightenment. Despite the derision, the symbol survived and it became one of the most identifiable corporate logos. The surest sign of success came as it spawned a plethora of imitators.

In December 2006, and just weeks after its ten-year anniversary, the Innovation Ring was unceremoniously dumped. Lucent Technologies had merged with Alcatel to create Alcatel-Lucent, a global telecom equipment giant, and the combined entity unveiled a new corporate image. Devised, yet again, by Landor Associates, the new symbol features a stylised combination of the initials A and L. The two letters are joined at both ends to resemble an infinity symbol, and housed in a shiny button or bloated glyph – a graphic expression devoid of its predecessor's adventure or trend-setting potential, and that bears all the characteristics of Web 2.0 graphics.

152

DSM 'HEXAGON' 1969–2011

DESIGN: WERKGROEP NOVIVORM (NL)

DSM, an acronym of the company's original Dutch name, De Nederlandse Staatsmijnen (Dutch State Mines), was established in 1902 as a state-owned coal mining company. Through the years, DSM diversified into chemicals and by 1965, had completely phased out the mining operations.

As diversification accelerated in the late 1960s, DSM embarked on a rebrand process. This period is regarded by many as the Golden Age of Dutch corporate identity: a time when the industry champions Albert Heijn, NS, SHV and KLM adopted shiny new logos. Remarkably, all have survived virtually untouched. However, in contrast to these examples, DSM choose to create their new image internally, by a dedicated house style team led by graphic design luminary Pieter Brattinga.

After a design process of almost three years, and over 1,500 sketches, the new corporate identity was launched on December 3rd 1969. The cornerstone of the program was an abstract geometric symbol that evoked a stylised molecule, a benzene ring or a 3-D cube. DSM explained that the 'Hexagon' was "the most well-known chemistry symbol" and "an allegory of their core-activity, and the field in which they are expanding".[67] The symbol was the antithesis of the previous logo (an illustrative emblem showing three cooling towers contained within a circle); and a graphic form that signalled efficiency, innovation and a forward-thrusting dynamism.

Although DSM would become part of the wave of geometric abstracts that transformed international corporate symbology, it was the mark's application that was revolutionary. The device was accompanied by a comprehensive and monolithically imagined design manual entitled *Novivorm* (Normalisatie Visuele Vormgeving, or Visual Design Standards): a 120 page tome that stringently outlined in great detail all possible outings.[68]

By 2011, DSM had come a long way from the bulk chemical business it was 40 years earlier; and was now a multinational corporation specialising in "Life Sciences & Materials Sciences". It decided on a rebrand to soften and humanise its image; and to move on from corporate expression based on the rational, and perhaps cold, modernist orthodoxy. The new logo (devised by Coley Porter Bell) consists of a multi-coloured form that swirls around a hexagon-shaped void: a ghostly homage to the 1969 design.

153

HOECHST
'TOWER AND BRIDGE'
1951–1997
DESIGN: UNKNOWN

Hoechst was one of the world's premier industrial chemical companies during the 20th century. Founded in 1863 as a plant to manufacture dyes from coal tar in the city of Höchst, Frankfurt-on-Main, Germany, the company became a global leader in plastics, synthetic fibers and pharmaceuticals.

After World War II, the massive conglomerate IG Farben (a merger of six German heavyweights including BASF, Bayer, Agfa and Hoechst) was split into its founder companies. In 1947, as a signal of the restructuring, Hoechst introduced a new corporate emblem that featured its historic headquarters, in a symmetrical representation. Contained in a circle was a highly stylised contour of the distinctive tower and bridge of the listed *Behrensbau* (or Behrens Building) – an expressionist building from 1924 named after Peter Behrens, its illustrious architect who is viewed as a pioneer of modern corporate

identity (e.g. AEG) and the founder of German Modernism.[69]

In 1951, the Hoechst trademark was tweaked to the more familiar layout, when the tower was moved to the left side, while the bridge rose to the right to house the name of the company. For nearly 50 years, the idiosyncratic 'Tower and Bridge' logo remained virtually the same (albeit with some minor stylistic alterations, most notably the addition of a square framing device in 1960). It was at the heart of a unified modernist design aesthetic, that included a rigorous Helvetica-based typographic system.

By 1997, as Hoechst shed much of its chemical divisions and morphed into a 'life-sciences' company, it replaced its logo with an unremarkable wordmark: the name Hoechst set in the typeface Helvetica, embellished with a small blue square. The rationale explained that the new logotype (by Hans Günter Schmitz) better represented the bold and confident statements that the company wanted to make in relation to quality, innovation and growth. Furthermore, Hoechst wished to signal that it was a global company rather than a parochial one, as depicted by the Behrens building in Frankfurt. The result was another example of the culturally-imposed brand conformity that was creeping into almost every market sector.

With massive consolidation in the pharmaceutical industry, Hoechst merged with Rhône-Poulenc to form Aventis in 1999 – and with it, another distinguished brand name was consigned to the history books.

METLIFE 'FOUR MS' 1964–1990s

DESIGN: SANDGREN & MURTHA (USA)

MetLife, a non-initial abbreviation for Metropolitan Life Insurance Company, is the largest life insurer in the United States. In 1964, MetLife replaced its famous old tower logo and slogan, 'The Light That Never Fails' (which had existed since 1909), with an abstract symbol – designed by the unassuming talent of Don Ervin, of New York design agency Sandgren & Murtha. The symmetrical geometric form, created by rotating the initial 'M' four times at right angles, conveys qualities of strength and solidity needed by a financial institution. The visual distinctiveness of the logo is enhanced by the dynamic star-like activity that occurs within the negative space.

Ervin's logo was designed to give the "gray lady of insurance companies" a contemporary look – and is a typical example of the stern Modernist approach embraced by much of corporate America in the 1960s. Then, a good visual identity was a sign that would best convey the status and ambition of a company in a purely abstract way. Limitless geometrical shapes and primary colours abounded, contrasted only by endless arrays of acronyms set in a sans-serif typeface, usually Helvetica.

By the 1980s, these identities appeared somewhat forbidding. The public's perception of insurance and financial companies had changed. They were seen as distant, monolithic and soulless institutions – ready to grab your money. MetLife was no exception. "It wanted to appear friendly and caring but instead was perceived to have the personality of a life insurance company: faceless, bureaucratic, and cold."[70]

In 1985, in an effort to give its brand more 'emotional' value, MetLife introduced Snoopy, and other characters from the popular Peanuts comic strip, in its advertising campaigns. These cartoons were seen as the perfect solution to soften its corporate image, and to differentiate MetLife from its competitors. As the 1990s progressed, the MetLife logo was shuffled sideways and then completely phased out, replaced ignominiously by Snoopy as the corporate mascot.

Nowadays, the four radiating 'Ms' can still be seen on the east and west faces of the MetLife Building in New York (the last tall tower erected in NY before laws were enacted that prevented placing corporate logos and names on the tops of buildings). It is a reminder of the durability, elegance, impact and omnipotence of Ervin's design.

ARSENAL FC 'VCC CREST' 1949–2002

DESIGN: UNKNOWN

Football clubs, in general, have always had some of the key ingredients of branding – the team strip and fan loyalty. However, it wasn't until the 1990s, that these were managed on a professional basis to create a true brand and maximise merchandising potential.

Since 1922, Arsenal's official badge featured a single cannon – a reference to the formation of the club by a group of workers at the Woolwich armaments factory in 1886. Over many years, this motif developed into a pseudo-heraldic crest; and by 1949, it incorporated the word Arsenal and a scroll inscribed with the club's newly-adopted Latin motto 'Victoria Concordia Crescit' (or 'Victory Comes Through Harmony'). The coat of arms of Islington and a pattern of ermine were also added. Despite being the official emblem, the 'VCC crest' was only worn on the famous red and white shirts for the first time at the start of the 1990–91 season.

In 2002, 'the Gunners' unveiled a simpler, more modern crest as part of a major shake-up of the club's corporate image. The new design, by London-based 20/20, retained the famous Arsenal cannon but it now pointed right instead of left. Arsenal chairman Peter Hill-Wood insisted that the move was an attempt to combine the club's tradition with a forward-looking approach.[71]

The real reason for the change was that Arsenal were unable to copyright the VCC crest, as there is uncertainty surrounding its exact origin. With the new design, the club now have a single graphic standard – and, thus, more comprehensive legal protection.

The notion of ownership was evoked during a much publicised legal battle in which Matthew Reed, a street trader and life-long Arsenal fan, had defended his right to continue selling 'unofficial' Arsenal merchandise. He argued unsuccessfully that the use of a club crest was 'a badge of allegiance', and that it belonged to the supporters.[72]

The restyled badge provoked a negative reaction from fans, who booed during the official launch. They saw the old crest as the symbol of 'their' club and felt that the changes were too draconian and introduced without consultation. According to one passionate fan: "The crest is the heart of the club, not only does it lead you in everything that you do, but even its positioning on the shirt would have you believe that it helps to pump life into your body. Well Arsenal, the day I saw our new crest, my heart broke."[73]

COMMODORE 'C'
1962–1994
DESIGN: UNKNOWN

Commodore International Ltd. started life as a small typewriter sales and repair shop in Toronto, Canada. It was founded in 1958 by Jack Tramiel, a Polish emigré. Apparently, he chose 'Commodore' as he wanted a name with a naval ring and because higher ranks, such as General and Admiral, were already taken. Down the years, Tramiel's company pioneered and popularised so much of the technology we use today.

Introduced in 1962, the Commodore logo was a single letter 'C' linked with a red and blue burgee flag – a swallow-tailed flag, or pennant, which is generally used to denote the rank of Commodore in the navy. In some circles, the logo was affectionately nicknamed the 'chicken-head'.

During the 1960s and 1970s, the compact C logo featured on best-selling business devices such as adding machines, typewriters and electronic calculators. However, it was not until 1982, with the release of the Commodore 64 (C64), that the logo became one of the most recognisable in the world. Parents bought this home computer for their children as an educational tool, but disguised beneath its chunky keyboard were two features that invited other uses. As the first personal computer that could generate high-res graphics and great sound the C64 was perfect for playing games. Titles such as *The Last Ninja* and *Elite* were big favourites and the inspiration for much of today's Playstation Generation.

In its heyday, from 1983 to 1986, Commodore enjoyed absolute dominance of the home computer market. In fact, the C64 is the best-selling single personal computer model of all time.[74]

However, Commodore failed to understand the true nature of the personal computer industry and the power of marketing. By 1987, IBM had captured the market and Bill Gate's *Microsoft Windows* was beginning its conquest. The company tried to respond but it was too late, and in 1993, it reported crippling losses of $357 million. The following year, Commodore declared bankruptcy and it was finally *Game Over*.[75]

In early 2011, Commodore was relaunched as a niche retro brand. Nostalgic geeks and enthusiasts can buy a C64 emulator and games in Apple's App Store. The resurrection of this well-loved brand reveals the enduring equity and credibility of defunct names, and the simple fact that brands never really die (see page 176).

PTT POST
1989–1998

DESIGN: STUDIO DUMBAR (NL)

On January 1st 1989, the house style for the newly-privatised Dutch postal service 'PTT Post' was launched. The new identity, designed by Studio Dumbar, was part of an integrated design scheme for the holding company Royal PTT Netherlands (KPN) and its Post and Telecom divisions.

The logotype of PTT Post was composed of the letters 'P T T' in a modified Univers 65 typeface set in white, within a red square box. Adjoining the box was a rectangle with the division title and a row of five dots, that suggested the postal process, or the perforation of stamps. Although this typographical logo is rather rigid and unremarkable, it was the fulcrum of a celebrated corporate identity scheme.

Studio Dumbar specified that the house style did not have to be applied dogmatically and unimaginatively, provided that the design of the items in question met the highest professional standards. They explained that it was not the logotype that formed the main component of the corporate design, but the basic shapes derived from it: the lines, dots and squares. The resulting patterns resembled something of De Stijl; and the different geometric extrapolations decorated post offices, parcels, vehicles, trains, brochures and uniforms.[76]

Over the years, the playfulness of the PTT Post identity would evoke equal measures of admiration and criticism. Some saw the designs as little more than empty decoration, whilst others celebrated its graphic vitality and anarchy. According to design critic Rick Poynor: "The identity's presence as an ordinary part of life, encountered wherever you turn, contributes to a culture of possibility in which other kinds of freedom and experimentation can also flourish."[77]

In 1998, the telecommunications market in Europe was deregulated. KPN was split, with its Post and Telecom divisions continuing as separate independent entities. With both companies requiring new distinct identities, the pioneering house style of PTT Post was dropped. Studio Dumbar, who were once again chosen for the mammoth task, discarded much of its predecessor's playfulness and created a simpler design solution that was noted for consistency rather than adventure.

Unbelievably, considering its long commitment to the patronage of design, the Dutch postal services has undergone three rebrands since 1998: from 'TPG Post' (2002) to 'TNT Post' (2006) and 'PostNL' (2011).

AT&T 'GLOBE'
1984–2005

DESIGN: SAUL BASS/G. DEAN SMITH (USA)

With the 1983 court-ordered divestiture of the Bell operating companies, AT&T required a new visual identity and returned to Saul Bass, who had designed the Bell System identity in 1969. For more than five decades, Saul Bass was the doyen of big American corporate identity schemes and the undisputed master of film title design.

Under the art-direction of Bass (then of Bass/Yager & Associates), designer G. Dean Smith created one of the most iconic trademarks of the 20th century. The AT&T symbol, a solid circle crossed with lines modulated in width to create the illusion of dimensionality, suggested a "world girdled by information" (a phrase that Bass acknowledged predated the phenomenon of the 'Information Superhighway' by ten years).[78] The striated sphere signalled to AT&T customers, shareholders and employees that its new vision was international – a network spanning the world. Like much of Bass's work,

the symbol distills several complex ideas and associations into a beautifully simple, memorable and well-crafted piece of design. Over 20 years, the AT&T logo became as pervasive as the Coca-Cola signature, and was fondly nicknamed 'The Death Star', due to its similarity to the space station in Star Wars. In 1999, it was modified by Interbrand to include a subtle shadow and fewer modulated lines.

If judged by Bass's own criteria, the AT&T Globe is one of his finest: "the ideal trademark is one that is pushed to its utmost limits in terms of abstraction and ambiguity, yet is still readable. Trademarks are usually metaphors of one kind or another. And are, in a certain sense, thinking made visible."[79]

In 2005, AT&T was acquired by SBC Communications. The merged company rebranded as AT&T Inc. and unveiled a stylistic update of the globe (once again devised by Interbrand). Sadly, the semiotic swagger of the press release (which claimed that the redesign signals vitality, change and transparency) cannot disguise the failings of the new logo, which is poorly executed and incoherent. Many in the designworld saw the retirement of Bass's globe as ill-judged and a regressive step. In a touching eulogy, Michael Bierut (design luminary and critic) noted "Graphic design, unlike architecture, leaves no footprint. When one of the best known logos in the world disappears overnight, the only hole created is in our collective consciousness. By New Year's Eve, Saul Bass's sphere will be no more. Will anyone mourn, or protest, its passing?"[80]

159

MIDLAND BANK 'GRIFFIN' 1965–1997

DESIGN: PETER PICKARD (UK)

For much of the 20th century, Midland Bank was one of the Big Four banks in the UK – the others being Barclays, Lloyds and National Westminster. Despite its size, it had a reputation as a friendly bank and innovated the concept of retail banking in Britain. It was the self-titled "Listening Bank".

In 1965, Midland Bank launched a logo that was to become an ever-present symbol on the UK High Street for more than three decades. The logo was designed by Peter Pickard and consisted of a stylised prancing 'Griffin' – surrounded by a circle of 22 golden coins (or guineas), that represented the amalgamation of 22 banks.

The Griffin was an appropriate visual metaphor for a bank. Since medieval times, this mythical beast has represented strength and vigilance. Possessing a lion's body and the head and wings of an eagle, the griffin combined the qualities of the king of beasts and the king of the birds. It was also seen as a guardian of treasure; reputed to be able to discover and hoard gold. On launch, the bank aired a series of memorable TV adverts entitled 'Money Talks' directed by the legendary designer Robert Brownjohn.

By the 1980s, after a spate of unsuccessful flirtations abroad, Midland Bank refocused on its core domestic banking business and rejuvenated its corporate image. In 1986, the bank unveiled a restyled Griffin, designed by Chong Huang Tay of Wolff Olins.

In 1993, the Midland Group was bought by HSBC (Hongkong and Shanghai Banking Corporation), one of the world's largest financial services organisations. By April 1997, Midland Bank had adopted its parent's brand name. The ubiquitous gold-on-blue Griffin was ruthlessly slain and replaced with the red and white hexagon symbol of HSBC (the red 'bow-tie', designed by Henry Steiner).

The replacement of local banking brands, such as Midland and Abbey National *(see page 171)*, by global ones might meet with approval in the boardroom, but in the High Street, these new brands are sometimes perceived as soulless, generic and distant. In the bid to go international, the designs are often neutralised and sadly lacking in personality, or local character. As Marcel Knobil, chairman of Superbrand, said, "I think it has been difficult to maintain the sense of warmth that the Griffin had. The Griffin was a chat over the fence, whereas HSBC is more a chat over the Atlantic."[81]

HTV
'AERIAL'
1970–1992

DESIGN: HARLECH HOUSE (UK)

Harlech TV was born on March 4th 1968. The station was named after Lord Harlech, a former ambassador to Washington, and was backed by many of his famous friends including Stanley Baker and Richard Burton. Promising to broadcast two-thirds of its programmes in the Welsh language, Harlech was a proud and important catalyst in the revival of the Welsh cultural identity. In fact, many viewed it as the national broadcaster for Wales.

In 1970, the station changed its name to HTV to placate viewers in the West of England. Echoing this change, the station introduced a new logo – a form that robustly links the HTV initials to suggest a television aerial. It is self-contained and versatile, and makes good use of an appropriate visual pun (during this time, there was an unsightly antenna attached to the majority of homes).

The HTV logo allowed for two variations to convey its dual region franchise: HTV 'Cymru Wales' (Welsh language) and HTV 'West' (English language). The continuous angular lines, rendered in white on a blue background, remained at the heart of HTV's on-air presentation for 22 years. Usually, it was animated in a short sequence of thick strokes and accompanied by a slightly hypnotic jingle called the 'Waterfall'.[82] It was one of the most memorable and pioneering channel logos, or idents, of the 1970s and 1980s; and had a profound impact on television graphic design.

HTV produced a prodigious amount of programmes – churning out more than any other regional company. On the ITV network (independent/non-BBC), the distinctive Aerial was a regular sight on British and Irish television screens.

With relaxed regulations and the start of a new franchise period in the 1990s, Granada and Carlton (two of the larger independent broadcasters) began to absorb all the others. In their efforts to cut costs and raise corporate awareness, the unique regional nature of ITV was stripped away. Many endearing idents such as LWT, Anglia, Thames and HTV were discarded. On December 31st 1992, the HTV Aerial was abruptly removed; and replaced with a shiny new generic ITV brand – that signalled the start of a Digital Age, and confirmed the homogeneity of the TV landscape.

In October 2002, HTV as an 'on air' brand disappeared completely in a major revamp of ITV presentation and continuity.

PYE 'ROUNDEL'
1947–1988
DESIGN: UNKNOWN

Pye was founded by William George Pye in 1896. Under the chairmanship of Charles Stanley, the company was transformed from a small Cambridge instrument maker into a worldwide electronics giant, with over 30,000 employees. It was a pioneer producer in Britain of domestic radios in the early 1920s, televisions in the 1930s, and transistor radios in the 1950s.[83]

From 1927, the speaker grilles of all Pye radios were cut in the shape of a *rising sun*, a motif that was extremely popular and reflected the contemporary taste for Art Deco. In 1938, the Pye name was incorporated into the design; with the letter 'Y' centred to echo the radiating sun rays. Soon after the end of World War II, Pye was forced to amend this fretwork motif, as it was deemed too similar to the flag of Imperial Japan. In 1947, a streamlined version, consisting of a solid black circle superimposed by angled white letter-forms was introduced. Uniquely, it doesn't try to mean anything. The mark, a model of economy, simply fosters instant recognition, by utilising the inherent graphic dynamism and symmetry of the letter 'Y'.

Throughout the 1960s, Pye was as ubiquitous in Britain as Sony is today. Besides domestic electronics, the roundel was synonymous with chart-topping records. The logo adorned the releases of The Kinks, The Searchers, Sandy Shaw and David Bowie – usually at the centre of a distinctive pattern of concentric circles. Together with EMI and Decca, Pye was part of the triumvirate of great British labels in the 1960s heyday of pop music.

However, whilst Pye records was constantly *delivering the hits*, its parent company got into difficulties. Pye did not respond adequately to the increasing competition from Japan – which had flooded the market with cheap radios and cut-price televisions. By 1976, the Pye group of companies was bought outright by Philips; and their subsequent rationalisation of activities saw the slow phasing out and debasing of the Pye brand.

One of Pye's last forays into consumer electronics was 'The Pye Tube Cube', in 1982: a device that combined a clock radio, cassette recorder and TV. However, it failed to catch the imagination of the public. After nearly a century at the heart of British households, Pye ceased trading in 1988. The once omnipresent brand was switched off for good.

the idea. "Every job has to have an idea. Otherwise it would be like a novelist trying to write a book about something without really saying anything."[84] The logo, which survived some minor alterations over three decades, has long been touted as one of the most identifiable, evocative and enduring trademarks ever.

However, with the advent of the internet in the late 20th century, Reuters sought a redefinition of its brand. It embarked on transforming itself from a global news agency into a global business information provider. Central to this development was a subtle change to Fletcher's logo and the addition of the day/night symbol (a roundel composed of dots), by Enterprise IG in 1996. Three years later, the dotted logotype was dropped completely and replaced with a solidified wordmark. Reuters explained that Fletcher's logo "was too redolent of old-fashioned telex ticker-tape. Worse still it failed to stand out, particularly on video-screens..."[85]

Many in the design community disagreed. According to Paul Postma, the axing of the dotted logotype was a shame. "They had a first-rate logo. Now, it is a compromise... it needs an extra element to say what previously it had said with just seven letters."[86]

In 2008, Reuters underwent another dramatic rebrand after it was acquired by Thomson to form Thomson Reuters. The new symbol, devised by Interbrand, is composed of a spiral of dots, and allegedly "leverages the equity of the Reuters dots."[87]

REUTERS 'DOTTED LOGOTYPE' 1965–1996

DESIGN: CROSBY/FLETCHER/FORBES (UK)

Reuters was founded in London in 1851 by Paul Julius Reuter, who began dispatching information from one place to another by carrier pigeon. By the 1960s, Reuters was one of the world's largest news services. As television was replacing newspapers as the most popular source of news, the company decided to have a new and distinctive face for their organisation.

In 1965, Alan Fletcher, then at Crosby/Fletcher/Forbes (the forerunner of Pentagram), crafted an identity from the word 'Reuters' rendered in a basic grid of 87 dots to evoke the company's trade. The dotted letterforms were inspired by the holes in teleprinter tape, which was then the primary medium for the global transfer of news reports.

The logotype is typical of Fletcher's penchant for creating witty and elegant work – and is a testament to his conceptual timelessness. In fact, nothing was as important to him as

163

FESTIVAL OF BRITAIN 'BRITANNIA' 1948–1951

DESIGN: ABRAM GAMES (UK)

100 years after the Great Exhibition in Crystal Palace, the Festival of Britain was hosted on London's South Bank. From May to October 1951, this fantasy world, built on 27 acres of cleared bomb sites, attracted some ten million visitors. It was a celebration of British culture and a perfect 'tonic to the nation'[88] during its recovery from war.

Three years previously, twelve* of the most respected British designers of the day were invited to participate in a competition to design an emblem for the festival. The brief stated that "the symbol must be simple in form, have popular appeal, and be readily recognisable". In addition, the symbol must also convey "a summer of gaiety and good looks."[89]

The winner was Abram Games, a designer more noted for his brilliant series of war posters. His original submission consisted of a stylised profile of Britannia (Britain personified as a classical female figure) surmounting the star of the compass, and typography that was a link back to the 1851 exhibition. However, after some criticism from the public that deemed the symbol too militaristic and lacking in gaiety, Games was invited to modify the design. Inspired by watching his wife hanging the washing, he added a half circle of festive bunting in red, white and blue.[90]

Formally, the festival emblem is bold, vigorous and gently humorous, and perfectly illustrates Games' personal maxim – "maximum meaning, minimum means".[91] It also reveals his talent in combining word and image into one powerful, aesthetic whole. Games went on to design the official postage stamp, guide covers and flags of the festival – yet, despite his reputation, not the official posters.

The Britannia emblem somehow captured the optimism and whimsy that was the spirit of 1950s Britain. In a colourless post-war period, the copyright-free Britannia emblem featured on an eclectic array of souvenirs and curios, which included tea-cups, posters, ashtrays, powder-boxes and flowerbeds. The Council of Industrial Design even suggested its long-term use as a 'Made in Britain' symbol. But many others in the design community were less impressed. They criticised the decorative illustrative style, the Victorian type-faces and their derivatives, and regarded the gaiety and colour of the festival as a retrograde step.[92]

---

* AMONGST THE 12 DESIGNERS INVITED WERE MILNER GRAY, FHK HENRION, THEYRE LEE-ELLIOTT AND TOM ECKERSLEY.

DELOREAN MOTOR COMPANY 'DMC' 1977–1983

DESIGN: DMC (USA)

A DeLorean motor car, with its gull-wing doors, rear mounted engine and stainless steel body panels, is an unforgettable sight. The unique design gives the car a futuristic look and is forever immortalised in the popular *Back to the Future* films of the 1980s.

The DeLorean Motor Company (DMC) was founded in 1975 under the direction of John Zachary DeLorean. DeLorean, who had been vice-president of General Motors, left the company to pursue his dream of designing the ultimate car that would bear his name. His goal was to produce a vehicle that would be safe, reliable, comfortable, fun to drive and definitely unmistakable.[93]

In 1981, DeLorean rolled out his self-styled 'ethical sports car' from a state-of-the-art factory in Northern Ireland. The car, the DMC-12, was a sensation. It was created by renowned Italian designer Giorgetto Giugiaro, and Colin Chapman, founder of Lotus.

Proudly mounted to the front grille were the initials 'D M C' rendered in a stripped-down, brash and futuristic typeface. The vignette can be described as a mirror-image ambigram. To some, it may conjure an unsophisticated or even high-school aesthetic, but it was just like the car it represented: robust, dynamic, uncompromising and cutting-edge. Besides, it was a highly distinctive badge in an automotive world full of circle abstracts and stylised animals. To create a more holistic brand image, the characteristic initials were developed into a complete DeLorean typeface.

However, within months of the launch, DeLorean's dream was embroiled in a quagmire of scandal and financial irregularities. Company sales were falling and DMC was in trouble. While John DeLorean was desperately searching for backers, he was arrested for drug trafficking. Even though he was exonerated from all federal drug charges brought against him, his reputation and credibility were devastated, and his new company was destroyed.

In February 1982, DMC was declared bankrupt. Under control of the British Government, the final cars were built in order to offset outstanding debt. In 1983, the DeLorean Motor Company closed its doors for good – and thereby bringing an ignoble end to a short-lived yet visionary design.

- **THE FIRST IMAGES OF THE DELOREAN FEATURED THE INITIALS 'DSV', STANDING FOR 'DELOREAN SAFETY VEHICLE', ON THE FRONT PANEL.**

BP 'SHIELD'
1930—2000
DESIGN: VARIOUS

For 70 years, the green and yellow shield of BP (British Petroleum) was one of the most instantly recognisable brand marks in the world.

The origins of the BP logo go back to 1920, when a staff competition to design a trademark was won by A. R. Saunders, an employee of the purchasing department. The winning design featured the initials 'B' and 'P' with wings on their edges, or hooked-serifs. In 1930, a heraldic shield was introduced to envelop this monogram.

Precisely how the famous colour palette of green and yellow came about is something of a mystery – but, according to BP, the colours inside the shield could be almost anything (red, blue, black, green, yellow, white) in the first decade.[94]

The BP Shield survived three major reincarnations (1947, 1958 and 1989) and throughout retained an author-itative presence that was steeped in history. Perhaps the most celebrated version of the logo was devised by the prolific designer Raymond Loewy in 1958. He eliminated unnecessary elements, strengthened the letterforms, and revitalised the colour scheme – as he saw the original as rather "drab and uninviting". One last makeover occurred in 1989 when Siegel+Gale updated the shield and italicised the initials for added dynamism.

In 1999, BP and Amoco completed a $53 billion merger, to form BP Amoco. The new board decided that, rather than integrating under an existing image, they needed a new one to signal the birth of a global power brand, and herald BP's embrace of change. In the process, the venerable shield was unceremoniously discarded.

On July 25th 2000, BP unveiled a new emblem: the 'Helios', named after the sun god of ancient Greece. The sunflower symbol, with its interlocking planes and colours, is designed to show the company's commitment to the environment and solar power. Devised by Landor Associates, the mark evokes "natural forms and energy that represent, respectively, BP's position as an environmental leader as well as their goal of moving beyond the petroleum sector".[95] To reinforce this strategy, the initials BP were given a new explanation as 'Beyond Petroleum'.

At the time, much of the designworld and British press united in criticising the Helios symbol. In fact, since the *Deepwater Horizon* oil spill of 2010, there seems to be a misalignment between brand promise and brand reality that could take BP many years to recover.[96]

ROVER 'LONGSHIP'
1929–2005
DESIGN: VARIOUS (UK)

Rover was the last British-owned volume car maker, and is one of many defunct auto brands *(see 'Riley' page 139)*. Its origins date back to 1884, when cycle makers Starley & Sutton picked the moniker Rover for their special tricycle design, which they considered to be ideal for 'roving' the countryside. The name proved so popular that it was adopted as the company name. The earliest Rover cars were built in 1904; but it wasn't until 1922 that Rover's Viking theme began.[97]

As the word Rover means wanderer or seafarer, a Viking was considered a fitting mascot for the company. In the 1920s, a Viking head with winged helmet was used as a radiator cap figure and on the original triangular brandmark. In 1929, this was replaced with a Viking 'Longship'. The golden prow and burgundy-coloured billowing sails of the ship evoked Norse mythology, and appropriate associations such as adventure and exploration.

In the 1930s, Rover established a reputation for providing the middle classes with their wheels of choice. The landmark P4 design (of 1949), the so-called 'Auntie' Rover, cemented its somewhat sedate image in the market. The P5 (from 1958) was a favourite of the Queen, and was the car of Prime Ministers from Wilson to Thatcher. The association with British authority continued with the Rover 75 (from 1999) as the ministerial car of the Blair cabinet.[98] Consequently, the Rover marque epitomised traditional British style – just like a pin-striped suit, a red Routemaster bus and a bowler hat.

As the designs of the cars changed over the years, the Rover Longship was frequently reworked. David Bache, Rover's chief styling engineer from 1954–81, is probably responsible for the version that we know today.[99] In 1990, the badge was revitalised by Marketplace Design Partnership.

Despite a state-controlled absorption by the Leyland Motor Corporation in 1967 and subsequent mergers, nationalisation and de-mergers through the 1970s and into the 1990s, the Rover marque retained its identity. But, the schizophrenic culture was the beginning of the end. The company's heritage drowned beneath the infamous industrial relations and managerial problems that beset the British motor industry.

Rover company ceased trading in April 2005, with debts of over £1.4 billion. After a marathon journey, the Rover Longship finally faded across the horizon.

167

UNILEVER 'TWIN PILLAR U' 1969–2004

DESIGN: COLLIS CLEMENTS (UK)

Unilever came into force in 1930 after the fusion of the Dutch company Margarine Unie with the British soapmaker Lever Brothers. Over subsequent decades, the Anglo-Dutch firm expanded into a multinational corporation that developed and acquired many of the world's foremost consumer product brands in foods, beverages, cleaning agents and personal care products (e.g. Axe, Flora, Lipton, Lux and Omo).

Since its foundation, the corporate signature of Unilever was a rather benign and clichéd 16-point Compass Rose (an emblem on maps that indicates the direction of north, south, east and west) that integrated the company name. After a period of takeover mania in the late-1960s that redefined its vast empire, Unilever sought a more contemporary and unified look. In 1967, Design Research Unit (DRU) was invited to reassess Unilever's corporate projection. After a process of 18 months, where "abstracts galore were created and then abandoned",[100] the designer Collis Clements devised a bold letter U. It's a symbol that expresses "the strength and stability of the business and demonstrates the twin pillars of Unilever joined to form an integrated whole."[101] This decidedly effective and visually acute trademark endured for almost 35 years (albeit with a slight refresh by Ken James in 1990).

However, there were times when Unilever appeared amorphous. Its corporate image, unlike its brands, remained hidden. The logo was not found on any products or advertising – as the prevailing wisdom was that its scale and scope made it vulnerable to criticism and that there was little to be gained by seeking a high public profile.

The 75th anniversary of Unilever prompted a brand overhaul fuelled by a strategic repositioning, significant for the recognition of the growing importance of the corporate brand. In short, Unilever decided to become more visible. The corporation ditched the rather industrial design of Collis Clements – and unveiled a new U (devised by Wolff Olins) that was more than just a single initial. Composed of 25 icons that represent different aspects of Unilever's business, the symbol conceptually supports and reflects the mission statement "to add vitality to life".[102] Despite the complex execution, the form is a harmonised whole that communicates in a more friendly tone.

BT 'PIPER'

1991–2003

DESIGN: WOLFF OLINS (UK)

During the 1990s many companies* swapped their abstract and stern Modernist logos for a narrative form that told a story rather than simply creating a recognisable presence. One of the first companies to reshape itself in this way was British Telecom.

In 1991, British Telecom was relaunched as the simpler and more international 'BT'. Central to the rebrand was a new corporate mark: the 'Piper', a stylised figure who was dancing and holding a trumpet. The figurative logo was a much friendlier presentation of its corporate identity than its predecessor, the partially dotted technological T in a circle (devised by Banks and Miles in 1980). The piper's pose of one hand to its ear and the other holding a large trumpet symbolised the listening and speaking concepts of communication. The dual contours in red and blue further emphasised this idea and highlighted the company's Britishness. The overall effect helped to express a change in BT's culture with renewed focus on customer service.

According to Wolff Olins, the new identity conveyed "BT's focus, the human communications business, with a symbol that can be understood across national borders. The figure of the piper is a universal image with roots in the folklore of many cultures. Listening as well as announcing, the image represents the company as responsive and accessible."[103]

For nearly 12 years, the 'prancing piper', as it was fondly dubbed, was an effective and ubiquitous brand ambassador. It appeared on over 70,000 vehicles and 60,000 phoneboxes, as well as bills, stationery and phone books. However, since its inception, the red and blue figure was almost universally ridiculed. Many in the designworld felt it was poorly drawn, whimsical and an obvious example of strategy driven design. Market research found it conjured up an arrogant image of BT as a company 'blowing its own trumpet' in consumers' minds.[104]

In April 2003, BT's Piper sounded his final call, and was replaced with the 'Connected World' symbol (also designed by Wolff Olins). According to the company, the adoption of this multi-coloured globe image "more accurately reflects the wide range of activities that BT now encompasses."[105]

---

* **AKZO (NL), PRUDENTIAL (UK) AND RABOBANK (NL) WERE PART OF A TREND FOR ANTHROPOMORPHIC IMAGES THAT INVADED THE CORPORATE IDENTITY LANDSCAPE IN THE 1990S.**

BRANIFF AIRWAYS 'BI' 1965–1978

DESIGN: ALEXANDER GIRARD (USA)

From its founding in 1928, Braniff International Airways (BI) was a modest airline with a steady and conservative rate of growth. This was all to change spectacularly in 1965 with the bold vision of the company's new president, Harding Lawrence.

Lawrence appointed the New York advertising agency of Jack Tinker and Partners to transform the company's image. Mary Wells, who managed the Braniff account, tapped into the talents of the renowned American graphic and interior designer Alexander Girard and the Florentine couturier Emilio Pucci. Wells' aim was to reposition the company from a regional carrier into a truly international airline.

Alexander Girard's design brief was vast. It included new schemes for the planes, uniforms, airport lounges, ticket offices and corporate logos. He also introduced, what remains to this day, a unique concept by having the fuselage

of each aircraft painted in one of seven vibrant colours: powder blue, medium blue, orange, ochre, turquoise, lemon yellow and beige.

Just as striking was the typographic logo on the tail fins. Rather than employing one of the usual clichés associated with flight, such as winged mammals, flying birds and globes, Girard created the italicised initials 'BI'. The bold letterforms were part of a proprietary typeface, created by John Neuhart and Karl Tani, that together with the bespoke fabrics and the moulded plastic furniture (prominent at ticket counters and lounges) achieved a consistent, integrated and compelling brand expression.

Overall, the brand makeover was a sensation. Braniff advertised that the new look in travel was literally taking off with "flying colours", and proclaimed the "end of the plain plane".[106] The retooled image suggested a fun, sexy and modern approach to air travel. It made Braniff a household name and increased business by a stunning 40% in the first year.[107]

In 1978, the 'Girard look' was deemed outdated. Company executives adopted an image that brought the airline into the Concorde Age – a mood that conveyed the urbane sophistication of the late 1970s. The 'Ultra look', as it was called, with its rich earth tones and sleek brown leather interiors was in stark contrast to Girard's bold exuberant style. Sadly, the stylised 'BI' logo was also dropped, and replaced by a script wordmark. After years of losses, Braniff filed for bankruptcy in 1982.

ABBEY NATIONAL 'UMBRELLA COUPLE' 1950S–2003

DESIGN: ERIC WINTER (UK)

For over half a century, a charming silhouette of a couple under an umbrella was one of the most familiar logos on Britain's High Street. The symbol signified the Abbey National Building Society (est. 1944), a former financial institution that specialised in mortgage lending.

Dated from the early 1950s, the original version of the Abbey National logo was a rather benign comic-book-style illustration of a strolling couple sheltering under a roof-shaped umbrella. The drawing was created by Eric Winter, an illustrator of children's books, most notably the Ladybird series. According to Winter, the inspiration for the odd-shaped roof was a house opposite his studio in Broxbourne, England.[108] By 1961, the illustration was redrawn and simplified to the more recognisable graphic form.

The adoption of an umbrella as a visual metaphor in the financial sector,

is a common ploy to communicate the concept of security and reliability. The Citigroup and the former Dutch insurance company RVS are just two other examples. Unlike these, the design of the Abbey National logo is somewhat naïve or vernacular. In fact, the untutored design beginnings of the mark delivered an unambiguously different, welcoming, helpful and customer-friendly message. An atypical approach that was amplified by popular 1970s advertising campaigns, such as 'Get the Abbey habit' that featured the logo contained within a thumb-up icon.

By the late 1990s, after a demutualisation process and an unsuccessful venture into the wholesale loans business, the Abbey National faced great difficulties. In a bid to revive the bank's flagging fortunes, chief executive Luqman Arnold declared that the institution was "turning banking on its head" by refocusing on the retail consumer.[109] In 2003, the brand name was shortened to Abbey and the bank adopted a soft, pastel-coloured logotype (by Wolff Olins). After enjoying a long and prosperous life, the couple with umbrella were forced into retirement.

Within 18 months, Abbey was cannibalised by Santander,[110] the giant Spanish banking group, who proceeded to rebrand all branches with their 'Flame' logo, and red and white livery (by Landor Associates). In January 2010, the Abbey name was ditched for good; thus bringing to an end, 66 years of financial heritage.

171

WELLCOME 'UNICORN' 1908–1995

DESIGN: UNKNOWN

Wellcome, originally 'The Burroughs Wellcome & Co.', was founded in 1880 in London by two American pharmacists, Silas Burroughs and Henry Wellcome. Almost overnight, their business was a huge success as they exploited the potential in developing and marketing compressed pharmaceutical products, (registered by the trademark 'Tabloid'), which were new to Europe.

To keep pace with the rapid growth in advertising at the turn of the 20th century, Burroughs Wellcome registered a stylised illustration of a unicorn as its trademark in 1908. The mythical creature, captured in an elegant trotting pose, can be classified as a metaphoric mark. Ever since medieval times, the unicorn was inextricably linked with the power to heal and cure; as its horn was believed to purify anything it touched.

By the 1950s, the motif was simplified

to a silhouette. Further stylistic changes were made in 1968, when the Unicorn was streamlined and locked together with a neutral sans-serif wordmark. Down the years, the distinctive blue Unicorn was central to Wellcome's brand image. It trotted gracefully across a variety of popular home remedies such as Kemadrin, Zovirax and Calpol. Spanning generations, the Unicorn became a beacon of comfort and reliance.

However, by the 1990s, a merger frenzy in the pharmaceutical industry took place. With rising research and development costs, drug companies realised that they were unable to go it alone (see 'Pharmacia & Upjohn' page 145, 'Hoechst' page 154). In 1995, rival company Glaxo took over Wellcome for £9 billion, to create the imaginatively titled 'GlaxoWellcome'. As the biggest merger in UK corporate history,[111] the new concern unified under a new wordmark, and the universally-recognised Unicorn was forced into extinction.

In 2000, the Wellcome name, once deemed sacrosanct in the history of pharmacy, disappeared from the drug business altogether when GlaxoWellcome merged with Smith-Kline Beecham, to form the moniker 'GlaxoSmithKline' (GSK). In fact, many other medical household names and their venerable logos simply vanished during this period – hidden or dissolved in mergers and acquisitions.

• THE WELLCOME NAME IS KEPT ALIVE BY THE WELLCOME TRUST, AN INDEPENDENT RESEARCH-FUNDING CHARITY.

PAN AM 'BLUE GLOBE' 1958–1991

DESIGN: EDWARD L. BARNES ASSOC. (USA)

Pan American World Airways was founded in 1927 as a scheduled airmail and passenger service operating between Florida and Havana.

In 1958, Pan American's traditional half-wing motif was replaced with a stylised globe – a symbol that consisted of a perfect circle intersected with curved parabolic lines. The new motif, devised by Joseph Montgomery of Edward L. Barnes Associates, sought to reflect the global scope of its routes at the dawn of the Jet Age – whilst also capturing the airflow patterns of high speed flight. The agency also truncated the corporate name to Pan Am, the company's snappy nickname, and devised a distinctive wordmark, set in a 'wind swept' type-style, in the centre of the globe. Further impact came from the generous use of royal blue, and white as the base colour. The result was an extremely modern and sophisticated image.

In 1971, the airline turned to the celebrated design agency of Chermayeff & Geismar to rejuvenate their visual identity. In fact, a young Ivan Chermayeff was part of the original design team at Edward L. Barnes[112]. Aside from restyling the globe symbol, they introduced a new wordmark set in Helvetica.[113]

For decades, Pan Am's globe symbol became synonymous with the prestige and glamour of air travel. It was one of the world's most recognised trademarks, on a par with Coca-Cola. According to official archives, it was the airline that helped define major events in the 20th century – "Pan Am brought The Beatles to New York, the troops to war and back, and the food to Berlin."[114] To many, a world without Pan Am was almost unimaginable. A futuristic vision of the air carrier was immortalised in two classic sci-fi movies: *2001: A Space Odyssey* and *Blade Runner*.

However, the 1980s heralded the beginning of the end for Pan Am. The fuel crisis, the recession, the deregulation of the airline industry, and bad management all contributed to an already precarious financial situation. In addition, the tragedy at Lockerbie caused transatlantic passengers to steer towards other carriers. In 1991, Pan Am filed for Chapter 11 bankruptcy, and made its final flight – bringing an inglorious end to a cultural and graphic design icon.

- IN 2011, THE PAN AM BRAND NAME AND GLOBE SYMBOL WERE REVIVED FOR A TV SERIES, AND A RETRO-FLAVOURED ACCESSORY COLLECTION.

UPS 'BOW-TIED PACKAGE' SHIELD
1961–2003

DESIGN: PAUL RAND (USA)

UPS, an acronym for United Parcel Service, is one of the world's largest package delivery companies. As a result, the UPS shield is one of the most seen and recognisable logos on the globe.

Back in 1961, UPS commissioned Paul Rand to restyle its shield, which had existed in various iterations since 1919. Rand transformed the logo into a modern image by streamlining the contours and introducing balanced Gothic lower-case letters. He then added an outline of a package with a bow on the top representing a crown. This addition reveals Rand's remarkable aptitude for creating logos that were humanistic, if not playful – and his genius in communicating the essence of a brand.

Rand also had unorthodox methods for testing his designs, such as using his eight-year old daughter. According to Rand: "when I did UPS... I said, 'Catherine, what's this?' and she said,

'That's a present, Daddy' – which was perfect. You couldn't have rehearsed it any better."[115] The UPS logo was the cornerstone of a comprehensive corporate identity program and endured without modification for 42 years.

In 2003, UPS unveiled a restyled logo. The shield was given a three-dimensional appearance and the string-wrapped parcel was removed. UPS explained that the redesign (by FutureBrand) reflected the changed nature of their business, that now embraced financial services and supply chain management. In short, UPS was 'more than a package company'.[116]

Considering the reverence for Rand, the restyle provoked much controversy and negative reactions. Many design critics were dismayed at the loss of another design classic; yet seemed blind to the inappropriateness of Rand's symbol for a global shipper. UPS noted that for several decades, they've rejected packages with strings, which jam the sorting machines.

Whatever the rights and wrongs of the change, the debate proved the strong emotional bond that people have to trademarks. A connection also evident in the rebrand speech by the UPS chairman Mike Eskew. More akin to an eulogy, he compared Rand's shield to an old friend: "The time has come to move on. After more than 40 years of honourable service, it's time for this old friend to retire with the grace and dignity it deserves. So, today, we're saying goodbye. But unlike most goodbyes, this is not an ending. Rather, this is a new beginning."[117]

"The report of my death
was an exaggeration."

Mark Twain, New York Journal,
June 2nd, 1897

LOGO R.I.P?

RESURRECTION

In the course of compiling *Logo R.I.P.*, our morbid quest for defunct logos encountered many setbacks. No sooner had we added to our selection, than we were forced to discard others. The iconic symbols of Atari, Centre Pompidou and the 'Tsurumaru' of JAL included in earlier drafts, were brought back to life after years of inactivity. Similarly, some of the logos from the first edition of the book have since been resurrected. Ben, a Dutch mobile network operator, was relaunched as a discount outlet for T-Mobile in 2008. The Adidas 'Trefoil' made a triumphant comeback as the symbol for Adidas Originals, the heritage sports line.

Furthermore, MG, one of the most famous marques in British motoring history, was recently resuscitated. Now under Chinese ownership, the company unveiled a brace of new models. After a similar hiatus, Polaroid is fashioning a return to prominence. Just like the phoenix, these brands have risen from the ashes – and, simply confirmed that logos never really die. Unlike those who make them, logos (and the brands that they represent) do not necessarily follow predictable, irreversible life-cycles.

All the aforementioned are lapsed legacy brands that have the potential to build on a strong historical and emotional foundation. Their stories show how many 'dead' brands are ripe for plucking, as marketers can plug into a consumer's taste for nostalgia. Their reactivation confirms that brands are one of the most valuable assets a company has. Brand equity – of which consumer recognition of logos is key – is one of the key factors which is attractive to any savvy investor. After all, the revival, rethinking or repositioning of a once-extinct brand is far less costly than launching anew.

Other logos make a return in other ways. The BR 'Double Arrow' *(see page 179)* is an example of how a symbol can transcend its original commercial use. Although initially designed at the behest of British Rail, it was adopted by the British Department for Transport as a universal symbol, or pictogram, to represent 'Train Station'.

ENDANGERED

In our study, we noticed many iconic logos with a reduced sense of purpose, or a less assured position than before. Trademarks that were once the focal point of a company's communications, but now relegated to a subordinate capacity. The Philips Shield, the BASF Spiral and the Hitachi emblem are three examples circling the drain of obsolescence. It seems (as noted throughout the book) that the propensity to adopt type-only, indistinct or unimaginative trademarks is favoured by more, and more, multinationals; in the belief that such designs perform better in an ever increasing globalised world.

Other endangered logos, or marks condemned to death-row, are the results of recent mergers or acquisitions. Take-overs have long heralded the end for well-known logos, as stakeholders wish to communicate a new message and signal change. The historic roundel logo of ICI, once the bluest of British blue chip companies, and the Sun Microsystems logo *(see page 180)* are only two examples of familiar trademarks facing an uncertain future, or the imminent threat of extinction.

BRITISH RAIL 'DOUBLE-ARROW' 1964–?

DESIGN: DESIGN RESEARCH UNIT (UK)

Following the fragmentation of the British rail industry due to privatisation in 1994, the iconic British Rail (BR) logo led a precarious life. For several years, it seemed that this symbol would be consigned to the logo graveyard. However, since its adoption by the British Department for Transport, it is now the *de facto* symbol for the train network across the UK.

The BR 'Double-Arrow', publicly launched in 1965, was designed by Gerald Barney of Design Research Unit (DRU). The symbol is officially described as a form composed of "two-way traffic arrows on parallel lines representing tracks."[118] Almost instantly, this self-contained, defiantly modern and highly visible logo gained status as a classic of graphic design.

The BR insignia provided the foundations for a truly thorough and pioneering corporate identity scheme. BR believed that design was an integral

part of its services, as it moved towards modernisation. "British Rail became the leader in a new wave in public design… all the way British Rail was the guiding spirit and midwife in the creation of better design standards in public transport."[119] The Double-Arrow symbol was applied to all aspects of business from train liveries and staff uniforms to Sealink car-ferries and the infamous 'BR sarnie'.

However, by the 1980s, the image of BR was heavily tarnished. Years of neglect due to a lack of investment had taken its toll. BR's trains were often dirty and late, and its symbol became synonymous with bad service, which led to nicknames like 'the barbed wire' or 'the arrows of indecision.'[120]

From 1994–1997, British Rail was dismantled and separated into several independently-operated companies. As each operator tried to establish an image, the branding of rail services lost consistency. The BR symbol was replaced by a spate of truly awful design solutions each representing the now schizophrenic and inefficient face of the British rail-network. A once integrated whole has become a patchwork of competing interests.

The continued use of the BR Double-Arrow immediately after privatisation had more to do with convenience than design; as changing it would have made obsolete all the road signage (by Jock Kinneir) using it to indicate railway stations. In recent times DRU's symbol has had a renaissance, and is proudly displayed on every station façade and every ticket.

SUN MICROSYSTEMS 'AMBIGRAM' 1982–?

DESIGN: VAUGHAN PRATT (USA)

Sun Microsystems Inc. was founded in 1982 by four Stanford University graduates: Andy Bechtolsheim, Vinod Khosla, Bill Joy and Scott McNealy. The name is an acronym for the 'Stanford University Network', a computer project developed over the previous year by Bechtolsheim. It wasn't long before the company developed into one of the kings of Silicon Valley, where it focused on network computing, designing and manufacturing its own software and hardware. The company's seminal achievement was the introduction of Java technology, the first universal software platform that enabled developers to write applications once to run on any computer.[121]

The idiosyncratic logo of Sun Microsystems was designed by Bechtolsheim's former professor at Stanford, Vaughan Pratt. The Professor Emeritus (who is regarded as one of the earliest pioneers in the field of computer science) devised a rotationally symmetric chain ambigram, by featuring four interleaved copies of the word sun. He achieved this by observing that the pairing of the letters 'U' and 'N' is similar to the letter 'S' in a perpendicular direction. Based on a 2x2 matrix, the arrangement implies a circuit board or computer network.

The original version of the Sun logo had the sides oriented horizontally and vertically, but the design was reworked a year later and tilted at an angle of forty-five degrees for added dynamism. The corporate colour was also changed from orange to lavender, or blue-purple. The bold simplicity of the symbol was offset by the addition of the wordmark 'Sun', set in an italicised classic typeface. Despite these subtle changes, the essence of Pratt's design endured. The intrigue, relevance and graphic strength of the symbol is notable considering it was conceived by one versed in the symmetries in mathematics – not graphic design. Pratt acknowledges that he has "a slightly artistic streak... but, his mathematical subconscious may well have had a say in the final outcome".[122]

When Sun Microsystems was acquired by Oracle Corporation in January 2010,[123] the public face of the Sun brand was jettisoned. For now, the amiable ambigram refuses to die – and is still visible (as a discreet lock-up with the Oracle logo) on some computer servers and workstations. At any rate, Oracle's dual brand strategy is only temporary – and the classic Sun logo seems destined for the logo graveyard.

REFERENCES

1   Bierut, Michael, 'The Final Days of AT&T',
     www.designobserver.com, October 29th 2005
2   Stowell, Scott, 'The First Report of
     the (Unofficial) Graphic Design
     Landmarks Preservation Commission',
     from *Metropolis Magazine*, May 2004
3   Wilbur, Peter, *Trademarks: A Handbook of
     International Designs*,
     Studio Vista/Reinhold Art, 1966
4, 5 'Speedbird still flies on' from *Design Journal*,
     No. 296, July 1st 1973, (P. 16)
6   Quinn, Malcolm, *The Swastika: Constructing
     the Symbol*, Routledge, 1995 (P. 4)
7   Richard Danne quoted in:
     Graphis Corporate Identity 1,
     Graphis Press, Switzerland 1989 (P. 163)
8   Johnson, Michael, *Problem Solved*,
     Phaidon Press, London 2002 (P. 143)
9   'Mission Control, We have a Problem',
     by RitaSue Siegel, from *Design Annual 43*,
     Communication Arts.
10   'P&G raises hell over Satan claim',
     Marketing Week, September 15th 1995
11   Fletcher, Alan, *Pentagram*,
     Phaidon Press, London 1993 (P. 136)
12   Brayer, Elizabeth, *George Eastman:
     A Biography*, University of Rochester Press,
     Rochester NY, 2006
13   'Updated Kodak Brand Mark',
     by Antonio Perez, Kodak Press-Release,
     www.kodak.com
14   'Enron unveils new advertising campaign
     and logo; Gears up to tackle challenges in
     changing energy industry', Press Release
     January 14th 1997, *www.enron.com*
15   Eichenwald, Kurt, *Conspiracy of Fools:
     A True Story*, Broadway, New York, 2005
16   Cruver, Brian, *Enron: Anatomy of Greed –
     The Unshredded Truth from an Enron Insider*,
     Arrow Books, London 2003
17   Fortune 500, May 2001, *www.fortune.com*

18   Haig, Matt, *Brand Failures – The Truth about
     the 100 Biggest Branding Mistakes of All Time*,
     Kogan Page, London 2003 (P. 186)
19   Eskilson, Stephen J.,
     Graphic Design: A New History,
     Laurence King, London, 2007 (P. 333)
20, 21 'Celebration or Commemoration?
     The Rise of the VOC' by Carin Tiggeloven,
     24th April 2002, *www.rnw.nl*
22, 24 Quoted in: 'Tarmac – A History',
     www.tarmac.co.uk
23   Quoted in: Blake, John and Avril,
     *The Practical Idealists, Twenty-five years of
     designing for industry*, Lund Humphries,
     London 1969 (P. 96/97)
25   Quoted in: "Poem", by Paul Rand,
     1977 Yale exhibition catalogue on
     Herbert Matter, *www.aiga.org*
26   Gentleman, David, *Artwork*,
     Ebury Press, London 2002
27   Quoted in: 'Fixed compass:
     David Gentleman talks about his
     identity design for British Steel',
     www.blog.eyemagazine.com, 20th March 2011
28   Quoted in: 'The Top 20 logos of all time:
     No. 12 – British Steel',
     Creative Review, April 2011, (P. 48)
29   Fletcher, Alan, *The Art of Looking Sideways*,
     Phaidon Press, London 2001 (P. 516)
30   Extract from 'Robertson's Golly' –
     Robertson's Press Release, August 2001
31   'Energie Noord West: Symboliek van
     het beeldmerk', BRS/Eden press-release
32   Riley advertisement from Sept. 1936;
     Robson, Graham, *Riley Sports Cars 1926-38*,
     G. T. Foulis & Co (Haynes Group); 1989
33, 34 '3M Worldwide: The Life and Times
     of the 3M Logo', *www.3m.com*
35   Nakanishi, Motoo, *Corporate Design Systems 1
     – Case Studies in International Applications*,
     Sanno, Tokyo 1979 (P. 7)

36 Ken Garland quoted in essay
'Hans Schleger as I remember him',
Schleger, Pat, *Hans Schleger – A life of Design*,
Princeton Architectural Press,
New York 2001 (P. 267)

37 'Xerox History', *www.xerox.com*

38 "Xerox hopes its new Logo doesn't
say 'Copier'", by Claudia H. Deutsch,
The New York Times, January 7th 2008

39 'Xerox Unveils Biggest Change
to Its Brand in Company History',
Xerox Press-Release, *www.news.xerox.com*

40 Marchant, Nick & Addis, Jeremy,
*Kilkenny Design – Twenty-One Years
of Design In Ireland*,
Lund Humphries, London, 1984,

41 'What's in a Name?',
Irish Computer Magazine, March 2001

42 Ogilvy, David, *Ogilvy on Advertising*,
Crown Publishers, New York 1983 (P. 126)

43 'Merged group prescribes new identity',
Design Week, August 25th 1995

44 'Reflectactions' by Lynda Relph-Knight,
Design Week, November 28th 1996

45 *Wall Street Journal*, February 4th 1996

46 'Monsanto's name radically modified' by
Julia Finch, *The Guardian*, Jan. 28th 2000

47 'All set for MEXICO 68', by Jake Brown,
from *Design Journal*, No. 237,
September 1st 1968, (P. 26–33)

48, 49 Pedro Ramfrez Vázquez quoted in:
'This is a 1968... This is Mexico',
by Carolina Rivas, Daoud Sarhandi,
Eye Magazine 56, Summer 2005

50 Steve Jobs quoted in:
Heller, Steven, *Paul Rand*,
Phaidon Press, London 1999 (P. 194)

51 Steve Jobs quoted in interview:
'Paul Rand and Steve Jobs', by Doug Evans
and Alan Pottasch of AMP Films, 1993

52 'NeXT logo book', sourced from:
'Paul Rand + Steve Jobs', by Steven Heller,
www.imprint.printmag.com, October 2011

53 Heller, Steven, *Paul Rand*,
Phaidon Press, London 1999 (P. 196)

54 'Another brick in the structure of NI
agreement', by Gerry Moriarty,
Irish Times, 17th October 2001

55 Parliament debate on the Patten Report
(Opposition Day),
www.parliament.the-stationery-office.co.uk

56 'Transamerica Company Profile',
www.transamerica.com

57 Mackintosh, Ian,
Encyclopedia of Airline Colour Schemes,
Airline Publications, London 1979

58 'Seen but not heard of: Don Ervin,
Graphic Designer', by Steven Heller,
*Baseline (International TypoGraphics
Magazine)*, No. 59

59 'Sony History: This is a revolution!',
www.sony.net

60 Haig, Matt, *Brand Failures – The Truth about
the 100 Biggest Branding Mistakes of All Time*,
Kogan Page, London 2003 (P. 28)

61 'Betamax finally laid to rest',
www.news.bbc.co.uk, August 28th 2002

62 Geoff Halpin quoted in 'Voxpop',
Design Week, August 16th 2001

63, 66 'Money, Magic, Light' by Will Novosedlik,
Eye Magazine 28, Summer 1998, (P. 54)

64 Lucent Case Study, *www.landor.com*

65 Landor's Patrice Kavanaugh quoted in:
'Creating the Identity for a $20 Billion
Start-Up.' *Design Management Journal* 8,
1997, (P. 20–25)

67 Bakker, Wibo, *Droom van helderheid:
Huisstijlen, ontwerpbureaus en modernisme
in Nederland: 1960–1975*,
010 Publishers, Rotterdam, 2011 (P. 205)

68   *DSM Nieuws*, No. 25,
December 3rd 1969, (P. 4)

69   'Hoechst', by Dr. Karsten Kilian,
Marken Lexikon, Lauda-Königshofen,
www.markenlexikon.com

70   Aaker, David A., *Building Strong Brands*,
Simon & Schuster, London 1996 (P. 148)

71   'Arsenal Unveil New Crest',
www.arsenal.com, February 2002

72   'Arsenal scores trademark victory',
www.guardian.co.uk, May 22th 2003

73   'Better Crest Forgotten' by Jackie Bass,
www.onlinegooner.com

74, 75 'Commodore: A Brief History',
www.commodore.ca, March 18th 2002

76   'Flexible Geometry (PTT: Studio Dumbar)',
by Hugh Aldersey-Williams,
Eye Magazine 1, Autumn 1990

77   Quoted in: 'Studio Dumbar: Function and
Pleasure', by Rick Poynor, *Design without
Boundaries*, Booth-Clibborn Publications,
London, 1998 (P. 64)

78   Quoted in: Bass, Jennifer and Kirkham, Pat
Saul Bass: A Life in Film & Design,
Laurence King, London, 2011 (P. 330)

79   Quoted in: Bass, Jennifer and Kirkham, Pat
Saul Bass: A Life in Film & Design,
Laurence King, London, 2011 (P. 281)

80   Bierut, Michael, 'The Final Days of AT&T',
www.designobserver.com, October 29th 2005

81   Marcel Knobil quoted in: 'HSBC to warm
up its brand identity' by Gary Thurtle,
Marketing Week, March 22nd 2001

82   'The Harlech House of Graphics',
www.hhg.org.uk

83   Frankland, Mark, *Radio Man:
the Remarkable Rise and Fall of C.O. Stanley
(IEE History of Technology Series)*,
Institution of Electrical Engineers, 2002

84   Alan Fletcher quoted in:
'Reputations: Alan Fletcher (EYE talks to
Pentagram's Ringmaster of Paradox)',
Eye Magazine 2, Winter 1991, (P. 8)

85   Gilmore, Fiona, *Warriors on the High Street*,
Harper Collins, London 2001 (P. 101)

86   Quoted in: 'Logoland: Koeweiden
en Postma over logos en alibis' –
Credits No. 01, 2001 (P. 46)

87   Designer Chris Campbell quoted in:
'2008 Identity Works, Thomson Reuters',
by Tony Spaeth, *www.identityworks.com*

88   Woodham, Jonathan M., *Twentieth-Century
Design, Oxford History of Art Series*,
Oxford University Press, 1997 (P. 120)

89   Games, Naomi, *A Symbol for the Festival*,
Capital Transport Publishing, 2011 (P. 10)

90   Games, Naomi, *A Symbol for the Festival*,
Capital Transport Publishing, 2011 (P. 20)

91   Tambini, Michael *The Look of the Century –
Design Icons of the 20th Century*, Dorling
Kindersley, London, 1999 (P. 399)

92   Blake, John and Avril, *The Practical Idealists,
Twenty-five years of designing for industry*,
Lund Humphries, London 1969 (P. 42)

93   Fallon, Ivan and Srodes, James,
*Dream Maker: The Rise and Fall of
John Z. DeLorean*, Putnam, New York, 1983

94   'BP brand and logo: A brief history',
www.bp.com

95   'BP Corporate Identity: Creating a
New Breakaway Brand on a Global Scale',
www.landor.com

96   'BP falls out of index of top 100 brands
after Deepwater Horizon oil spill'
by Mark Sweney, *The Guardian*,
September 16th 2010

97, 99 Young, Daniel,
Rover P6 Anthology: 1963–1977,
P4 Spares, London, 1989

98   'Sad demise of a very British motor car',
     by Sean O'Grady,
     The Independent, April 8th 2005

100, 101 Collis Clements quoted in
     'Clash of Symbols', *Design Journal*,
     No. 244, 1st May 1969, (p. 30)

102 'Adding Vitality to Business'
     (Unilever Case-Study),
     www.wolffolins.com

103 'BT: Britain Talking' (BT Case Study),
     www.wolffolins.com

104 'BT calls up a new logo in attempt
     to escape from 'arrogant' image'
     by Liz Vaughan-Adams,
     The Independent, April 8th 2003

105 'BT unveils new logo', April 7th 2003,
     www.bbc.co.uk

106 'Technicolor Modernism',
     by Christopher Hawthorne,
     Metropolis Magazine, January 2001

107 *Fortune* Magazine, August 1966 (p. 146)

108 'Ladybird Authors & Illustrators',
     The Wee Web, *www.theweeweb.co.uk*

109 'Abbey drops brolly in hope
     of brighter days', by Andrew Cave,
     The Telegraph, September 25th 2003

110 'The tricky art of corporate makeover',
     by Ian Fraser, *The Sunday Herald (Scotland)*,
     March 6th 2005

111 'Drug giants in their own right',
     www.bbc.co.uk, February 24th, 1998

112 Bateman, Steven and Hyland, Angus, *Symbol*,
     Laurence King, London, 2011 (p. 238)

113 Chermayeff, Ivan, and Geismar, Tom,
     and Haviv, Sagi,
     *Identify: Basic Principles of Identity Design in
     the Iconic Trademarks of Chermayeff & Geismar*,
     Print Publishing, New York, 2011 (p. 234)

114 'Pan Am History – The chosen instrument
     (1927-1991)', *www.panamhistory.com*

115 Paul Rand in interview with Steven Heller
     from: Heller, Steven, *Paul Rand*,
     Phaidon Press, London 1999 (p. 189)

116 'Building the Brand: Behind the Scenes',
     (Press Release), *www.ups.com*

117 Extract from the speech of Mike Eskew,
     UPS Chairman and CEO, New York, on the
     announcement of the UPS Brand Strategy,
     'UPS Unveils New Look' (Press Release),
     www.pressroom.ups.com

118 Mollerup, Per, *Marks of Excellence:
     The History and Taxonomy of Trademarks*,
     Phaidon Press, London 1997

119 Cousins, James, *British Rail Design*,
     The Design Council/Danish Design
     Council, London 1986 (p. 2)

120 Cotton, Michelle,
     Design Research Unit 1942-72,
     Koenig Books, London 2011 (p. 72)

121 'Sun Microsystems', Wikipedia,
     www.en.wikipedia.org

122 E-mail Correspondence between Vaughan
     Pratt and The Stone Twins, Stanford
     University, California, November 27th 2011

123 'Oracle buys Sun, becomes hardware
     company', by Stephen Shankland,
     January 27th 2010, *www.news.cnet.com*

The publisher and author apologise for any
errors or omissions in the above list.
If contacted they will be pleased to rectify
these at the earliest opportunity.

BIBLIOGRAPHY
SELECTED

Aaker, David A., *Building Strong Brands,*
Simon & Schuster, London 1996

Baer Capitman, Barbara, *American Trademark
Designs* Dover Publications, New York 1976

Berger, Warren, *Advertising Today*
Phaidon, London 2001

Blackwell, Lewis, *20th Century Type (Remix)*
Laurence King Publishing, London 1998

Blake, John and Avril, *The Practical Idealists,
Twenty-five years of designing for industry*
Lund Humphries, London 1969

Blik, Tyler, *Trademarks of the '60s & '70s*
Chronicle Books, San Francisco 1998

Booth-Clibborn, Edward, *The Best of British
Corporate Design,* Booth-Clibborn, London 1989

BR, *Railfreight Design Guide*
BR Board, London 1988

Brazendale, Kevin, *Great Cars of the Golden Age*
Crescent Books, London 1979

Broos, Kees and Hefting, Paul
Een Eeuw Grafische Vormgeving in Nederland
Atrium Publishing, Alphen aan den Rijn 1997

Church, Roy A., *The Rise and Decline of the British
Motor Industry,* London 1995

Conrad, Barnaby, *Pan Am: An Aviation Legend*
Woodford Publishing, New York 1999

Conradi, Jan, *Unimark International*
Lars Müller Publishers, Baden 2010

Cooper, Barbara, *The Speedbird Story*
Golden Pleasure Books, London 1962

Cousins, James, *British Rail Design*
The Design Council/Danish Design Council,
London 1986

Crosby/Fletcher/Forbes, *A Sign Systems Manual*
Studio Vista, London 1970

Cruver, Brian, *Enron: Anatomy of Greed –
The Unshredded Truth from an Enron Insider*
Arrow Books, London 2003

Dormer, Peter, *Design Since 1945*
Thames and Hudson, London 1993

Evamy, Michael, *Logo*
Laurence King, London, 2007

Evans, Judith and Cullen, Cheryl Dangel,
Challenging The Big Brands
Guinness Publishing, London 1993

Foley, John, *The Guinness Encycl. of Signs & Symbols*
Guinness Publishing, London 1993

Fletcher, Alan, *The Art of Looking Sideways*
Phaidon Press, London 2001

Fletcher, Alan, *Pentagram*
Phaidon Press, London 1993

Frankland, Mark, *Radio Man:
the Remarkable Rise and Fall of C.O. Stanley*
Institution of Electrical Engineers, London 2002

Friedl, Ott, Stein, *Typography: When, Who, How*
Könemann, Koln 1998

Friedman, Thomas, *The Lexus and the Olive Tree*
Harper Collins Publishers, London 2000

Games, Naomi, *Abram Games - His Life and Work*
Princeton Architectural Press, New York 2003

Gandt, Robert, *Skygods: The Fall of Pan Am*
William Morrow Publishers, New York 1995

Garner, Philippe, *Sixties Design*
Taschen, London 1996

Gilmore, Fiona, *Warriors on the High Street*
Harper Collins, London 2001

Graphis, *Graphis Annuals (Various)*
Graphis Press, New York/Zurich

Graphis, *World Trademarks: 100 Yrs. (Volume 1 + 2)*
Graphis Press, New York/Zurich 1996

Grauls, Marcel, *De Kroon op het Merk, Pioniers van Wereldmerken,* Uitgeverij Balans, Leuven 2002

Haig, Matt, *Brand Failures – The Truth about the 100 Biggest Branding Mistakes of All Time* Kogan Page, London 2003

Herdeg, Walter (ed.), *Graphis Annual (Various)* Graphis Press, New York/Zurich

Heller, Steven, *Paul Rand* Phaidon Press, London 1999

Heller, Steven, *The Swastika: A Symbol Beyond Redemption?,* Allworth Press, London 2000

Hine, Thomas, *The Total Package* Back Bay Books, New York 1997

Hollis, Richard, *Graphic Design: A Concise History* Thames & Hudson, London 2000

Huygen, Frederique, *Brits Design – Imago & Identiteit,* Museum Boymans-van Beuningen, Rotterdam 1989

Huygen and Hugues C. Boekraad, *Wim Crouwel – Mode en Module,* Uitgeverij 010, Rotterdam 1997

Ibou, Paul, *Logo World* Interecho Press, Belgium 1994

Ibou, Paul, *Banking Symbols Collection* Interecho Press, Belgium 1990

Igarashi, Takenobu, *World Trademarks + Logotypes III* Graphic-sha Publishing, Tokyo 1991

Johnson, Michael, *Problem Solved* Phaidon Press, London 2002

Kamekura, Yusaku, *Trademark Designs of the World,* Dover Publications, New York, 1981

Knobil, Marcel, *Superbrands: An insight into Ireland's strongest brands,* The Brand Council, London 2000

Kuwayama, Jasaburo, Zeichen, *Marken und Signets: 3000 Internationale Beispiele,* Callwey, Munich 1973

Lennon, David, *Arsenal in the Blood* Breedon Books, Derby 1998

Livingston, Alan and Isabella *The T and H Encyclopedia of Graphic Design + Designers* Thames and Hudson, London 1992

Loewy, Raymond, *Industrial Design* 4th Estate, London, 1979

Lost and Found Critical Voices in New British Design The British Council/Birkhäuser, London 1999

Lupton, Ellen and Miller, Abbott, *Design Writing Research – Writing on Graphic Design* Phaidon Press, London 1990

Mackintosh, Ian, *Encyclopedia of Airline Colour Schemes* Airline Publications and Sales, London 1979

Marchant, Nick, *Kilkenny Design: Twenty-One years of Design in Ireland,* Lund Humphries, London 1984

Mendenhall, John, *Early Modernism: Swiss and Austrian Trademarks 1920-1950* Chronicle Books, San Francisco 1997

McDermott, Catherine, *Twentieth-Century Design* Design Museum/Carlton Books, London 1998

McQuiston, Liz, *Graphic Agitation, Social and Political Graphics since the Sixties* Phaidon Press, London, 1993

McQuiston & Kitts, *Graphic Design Sourcebook* Quarto Publishing, London 1987

Minale, Marcello, *How to Design a Successful Petrol Station,* Booth-Clibborn Editions, London 2000

Mollerup, Per, *Marks of Excellence: The History and Taxonomy of Trademarks* Phaidon Press, London 1997

Moody, Ella (ed.), *Modern Publicity 36 –1966/1967* Studio Vista, London 1966

Moynahan, Brian, *The British Century* Random House, New York 1997

187

Myerson, Jeremy and Vickers, Graham Vickers, *Rewind: Forty Years of Design and Advertising* Phaidon Press, London 2002

McQuiston & Kitts, *Graphic Design Source Book* Quarto Publishing, London 1987

Nakanishi, Motoo, *Corporate Design Systems 1 – Case Studies in International Applications* Sanno, Tokyo 1979

Neuburg, Hans, *Graphic Design in Swiss Industry* ABC Editions, Zurich 1965

Niggli, *The New Graphic Art* Switzerland 1959

Nourmand, Tony and Marsh, Graham, *Film Posters of the 70's* Reel Poster Press, London 1998

de Nijs, Ronald (ed.), *The Image of a Company: Manual for Corporate Identity* SDU Uitgeverij, The Hague 1990

Ogilvy, David, *Ogilvy on Advertising* Crown Publishers, New York 1983

Pastoureau, Michel, *Heraldry: Origins/Meaning* Thames and Hudson, London 1997

Pedersen, B. Martin (ed.), *Graphis Logo 1* Graphis Press, New York/Zurich 1991

Pedersen, B. Martin (ed.), *Graphis Corporate Identity 1*, Graphis Press, New York/Zurich 1989

Pentagram: The Compendium Phaidon Press, London 1993

Pijbes, Wim (ed.), *Studio Dumbar: Behind the Seen* Verlag Hermann Schmidt, Mainz 1996

Pilditch, James, *Communication by Design: A Study in Corporate Identity*, Berkshire 1970

Poynor, Rick, *Design without Boundaries* Booth-Clibborn Publications, London 1998

Quinn, Malcolm, *The Swastika: Constructing The Symbol*, Routledge, London and New York 1998

Rand, Paul, *Design, Form, and Chaos* Yale University Press 1993

Ricci & Ferrari, *Top Symbols & Trademarks of the World: Annual 1979/1980* F.M. Ricci/Deco Press, Milan 1981

Schleger, Pat, *Hans Schleger – A life of Design* Princeton Architectural Press, New York 2001

Sedgwick, Michael, *Auto's uit de Jaren '50 en '60* Batteljee & Terpstra, Leiden 1984

Slater, Stephen, *The Complete Book of Heraldy* Anness Publishing, London 2002

Spencer, Herbert (ed.), *The Penrose Annual 1969 (Vol.62)* Lund Humphries, London 1969

Stevens, Harm, *Dutch Enterprise and the VOC* Walburg Pers, Amsterdam 1998

Tambini, Michael, *The Look of the Century - Design Icons of the 20th Century* Dorling Kindersley, London 1999

Watano, Matsuzaki, *Design for Public Institutions in The Netherlands*, Shigeo Ogawa, Tokyo 1989

Wilson, Charles, *The History of Unilever*, Cassell & Company, London, 1970

Whyte Andrew, *101 Great Marques* Guild Publishing/Octopus Books, London 1985

Wilbur, Peter, *Trademarks: a Handbook of International designs*, Studio Vista/Reinhold Art, London, 1966

APPENDIX
NEW IDENTITIES

    ... 3M

From left to right, top to bottom:
BA 'Speedmarque' (Interbrand); NASA 'Meatball' (James Modarelli); P&G 'Wordmark' (Peterson & Blyth);
Kodak (BIG); Tarmac (Enterprise IG); Corus (Enterprise IG); Nuon (Tel Design); 3M (Siegel+Gale);
Xerox (Interbrand); Eircom (Identity Business); Pharmacia (Crosby Associates); Police Service N. Ireland;
Transamerica; Alcatel Lucent (Landor Associates); DSM (Coley Porter Bell); Hoechst (Hans Günter Schmitz).

From left to right, top to bottom:
MetLife (Young & Rubicam); Arsenal FC (20/20); PostNL (VBAT); AT&T (Interbrand);
HSBC (Henry Steiner); ITV (Red Bee); Reuters (Interbrand); BP 'Helios' (Landor Associates);
Unilever (Wolff Olins); BT (Wolff Olins); Braniff (Cars & Concepts);
Santander (Landor Associates); GSK (FutureBrand); UPS 'Shield' (FutureBrand)

INDEX

Page numbers in *italic* denote colour plates

ACKNOWLEDGEMENTS

We would firstly like to express our sincere thanks to all the featured designers and companies for their cooperation. Only the active support of most of the persons included in this book, or of their heirs, has made it possible. We'd also like to thank the individuals who submitted suggestions and condolences since the first edition in 2003. There are too many to mention by name, but we would especially like to thank: Rudolf van Wezel (BIS) for his belief and commitment to our project, Gert Dumbar for his encouragement and infectious enthusiasm, Jonathan Bolger for his critical eye, and our Mam and Dad for their invaluable assistance. Thanks also to Adrienne Stone, Irene Stone, Ines Scheffers, Dick Bezem', and our clients who pay the bills.

Lastly, but most importantly, our thanks and love go to Marieke and little Sam for their remarkable support, understanding and fresh coffee.

We thank You, we praise You.
We find strength and courage to go on.

AMEN.

Declan and Garech Stone,
The Stone Twins
Amsterdam, May 2012

ABOUT THE AUTHORS
The Stone Twins is a creative partnership, based in Amsterdam. Founded by
twin brothers Declan and Garech Stone
(born Dublin, 1970), the agency is noted
for its concept-driven and engaging
solutions. The duo are also Head of the
Communication department at Design
Academy Eindhoven. *www.stonetwins.com*